Online Resources

Congratulations! You now have access to practical templates of the Business Communication concepts that you will learn in this book. These downloadable templates will help you implement your learnings in the real world and give you an in-depth understanding of the concepts. The templates include:

They are:

- Punctuation Checklist
- List of Common Grammatical Errors
- Presentation Visuals, Tools, and Applications (Apps) You Need to Know
- Reference Styles and Other Necessary Mechanics
- A Formal Email Template for Product Introduction
- A Cover Letter Template
- A Business Proposal Template
- A Chronological Resume Template
- A Sample Memo Template

I0130504

To access the templates, follow the steps below:

1. Go to www.vibrantpublishers.com
2. Click on the 'Online Resources' option on the Home Page
3. Login by entering your account details (or create an account if you don't have one)
4. Go to the Self-Learning Management series section on the Online Resources page
5. Click the 'Business Communication Essentials You Always Wanted To Know' link and access the templates

Happy self-learning!

This page is intentionally left blank

SELF-LEARNING MANAGEMENT SERIES

VIBRANT
PUBLISHERS

BUSINESS COMMUNICATION ESSENTIALS

YOU ALWAYS WANTED TO KNOW

A deep dive into the nuances of effective business communication

DR. ANNAMARIA BLIVEN

Business Communication Essentials You Always Wanted To Know

First Edition

Paperback ISBN 10: 1-63651-163-5
Paperback ISBN 13: 978-1-63651-163-4

Ebook ISBN 10: 1-63651-164-3
Ebook ISBN 13: 978-1-63651-164-1

Hardback ISBN 10: 1-63651-165-1
Hardback ISBN 13: 978-1-63651-165-8

Library of Congress Control Number: 2024931907

This publication is designed to provide accurate and authoritative information in regard to the subject matter covered. The Author has made every effort in the preparation of this book to ensure the accuracy of the information. However, information in this book is sold without warranty either expressed or implied. The Author or the Publisher will not be liable for any damages caused or alleged to be caused either directly or indirectly by this book.

Vibrant Publishers books are available at special quantity discount for sales promotions, or for use in corporate training programs. For more information please write to bulkorders@vibrantpublishers.com

Please email feedback / corrections (technical, grammatical or spelling) to spellerrors@vibrantpublishers.com

To access the complete catalogue of Vibrant Publishers, visit www.vibrantpublishers.com

SELF-LEARNING MANAGEMENT SERIES

TITLE	PAPERBACK* ISBN

ACCOUNTING, FINANCE & ECONOMICS

TITLE	PAPERBACK* ISBN
COST ACCOUNTING AND MANAGEMENT ESSENTIALS	9781636511030
FINANCIAL ACCOUNTING ESSENTIALS	9781636510972
FINANCIAL MANAGEMENT ESSENTIALS	9781636511009
MACROECONOMICS ESSENTIALS	9781636511818
MICROECONOMICS ESSENTIALS	9781636511153
PERSONAL FINANCE ESSENTIALS	9781636511849

ENTREPRENEURSHIP & STRATEGY

TITLE	PAPERBACK* ISBN
BUSINESS COMMUNICATION ESSENTIALS	9781636511634
BUSINESS PLAN ESSENTIALS	9781636511214
BUSINESS STRATEGY ESSENTIALS	9781949395778
ENTREPRENEURSHIP ESSENTIALS	9781636511603

GENERAL MANAGEMENT

TITLE	PAPERBACK* ISBN
BUSINESS LAW ESSENTIALS	9781636511702
DATA ANALYTICS ESSENTIALS	9781636511184
DECISION MAKING ESSENTIALS	9781636510026
LEADERSHIP ESSENTIALS	9781636510316
PRINCIPLES OF MANAGEMENT ESSENTIALS	9781636511542
TIME MANAGEMENT ESSENTIALS	9781636511665

*Also available in Hardback & Ebook formats

SELF-LEARNING MANAGEMENT SERIES

TITLE	PAPERBACK* ISBN
HUMAN RESOURCE MANAGEMENT	
DIVERSITY IN THE WORKPLACE ESSENTIALS	9781636511122
HR ANALYTICS ESSENTIALS	9781636510347
HUMAN RESOURCE MANAGEMENT ESSENTIALS	9781949395839
ORGANIZATIONAL BEHAVIOR ESSENTIALS	9781636510378
ORGANIZATIONAL DEVELOPMENT ESSENTIALS	9781636511481
MARKETING & SALES MANAGEMENT	
DIGITAL MARKETING ESSENTIALS	9781949395747
MARKETING MANAGEMENT ESSENTIALS	9781636511788
SALES MANAGEMENT ESSENTIALS	9781636510743
SERVICES MARKETING ESSENTIALS	9781636511733
SOCIAL MEDIA MARKETING ESSENTIALS	9781636512181
OPERATIONS & PROJECT MANAGEMENT	
AGILE ESSENTIALS	9781636510057
OPERATIONS & SUPPLY CHAIN MANAGEMENT ESSENTIALS	9781949395242
PROJECT MANAGEMENT ESSENTIALS	9781636510712
STAKEHOLDER ENGAGEMENT ESSENTIALS	9781636511511

*Also available in Hardback & Ebook formats

About the Author

Dr. AnnaMaria Bliven has worked as a business professional for over 30 years gaining experience in business development and management, business improvement, project management, time management, career development and advancement, business strategy, and in starting and sustaining for-profit and not-for-profit businesses.

As a seasoned business owner and a master at managing time, her goals are to share lessons and best practices for starting, sustaining, and succeeding in business ventures, and leveling up in career fields. To that end, she meets with clients regularly assisting them with achieving their career and business goals. Dr. Bliven started her career as a Certified Travel Consultant while in the Army National Guard and served a total of 26 years with combined service in the Army National Guard, Army, and Army Reserve in the career fields of music, human resources, education services, and career development.

She has an undergraduate degree in Communication from Arizona State University, a Master of Arts degree in Communication from West Virginia University, and a Doctorate in Business Administration from the University of Wisconsin-Whitewater. She also achieved her certification as a Global Career Development Facilitator in addition to becoming a college instructor. She is also the author of Business Plan Essentials You Always Wanted To Know, Entrepreneurship Essentials You Always Wanted to Know and Time Management Essentials You Always Wanted To Know.

What experts say about this book!

Topics such as employment communication, social media, and crisis communication make this book extremely valuable. The quiz and the summary at the end of each chapter are other value additions. The lucid way of writing the book makes it easy to comprehend for the Master's students of business and communication, and the practitioners of corporate communication, public relations, and brand communication at the initial stages of their careers. Many examples, largely from the Western world, clearly illustrate the points made. The book covers both introductory content and special content in a balanced manner.

**– Prof Ujjwal K Chowdhury, Vice President,
Global Media Education Council**

Dr. Bliven's book covers all of the main aspects of business communications and provides it in easily digestible chapters. I have taken many courses in business communications over the years and I wish I had this book to serve as a comprehensive summary on how to think about the proper communication activities needed for any business. This book is a must-read!

**– David Fogarty, Chief Marketing Analytics and Data and Technology Officer,
Evernorth Corporation**

"Business Communication Essentials You Always Wanted To Know" offers practical advice and real-world examples to navigate various aspects of business communication, from written correspondence to presentations. Its emphasis on practicality, coupled with accessible language and engaging examples, ensures relevance for readers of all levels. Whether you're a seasoned executive or a business student, this book equips you with the tools to thrive in today's dynamic business landscape.

**– Jangho Gil, Ph.D., Accounting Professor,
Monmouth University**

Table of Contents

Preface

According to Paul J. Meyer, *"communication—the human connect—is the key to personal and career success."*

Business Communication Essentials provides all the necessary information that an organization can use to transform how it communicates with both its internal and external stakeholders. What separates this book from other related business books out there is that it treats the core subject-matter of communication in business comprehensively by providing understandable and helpful examples.

The executives or managers of most organizations know quite well that they need to keep their employees engaged and often reach out to their suppliers, customers, investors, etc. However, the approaches some of them have been taking are ineffective. This could potentially set a company towards its downfall.

Company managers as well as departmental supervisors are fully aware that their professional success and that of their subordinates (or team members) hang on productive communication. This is why it makes sense to say that without well-structured internal and external communication, no company can achieve its corporate goals and fulfill its mission/vision.

This book simplifies the processes of business communication in a way that anyone who carefully goes through it can happily discover some secrets of conducting successful business communication.

Introduction to the book

Communication is a vital aspect of running a business/company. It is very important to connect all stakeholders through routine and effective business communication. This book shows you exactly how you could do that.

You will discover all the necessary tips to facilitate excellent communication between your company's internal and external stakeholders. More importantly, you will unearth various business communication approaches you can use to keep your team, suppliers, investors, etc. happy and committed.

After reading the entire book, you will be able to identify:

- The importance of business communication and its different methods and modes

- The importance of understanding your intended audience and the steps to achieve great interpersonal communication

- The core business messages and their respective characteristics

- The best practices for drafting, editing, and completing business proposals, reports, and presentations

- The usefulness of business communication in customer relationship management (CRM)

- The impacts of social media and other modern-day technologies in business communication, and

- The best process for managing business crisis communication

How to use this book?

This book can be used by anyone who wants to either learn about business communication or improve their business communication strategy. Here is how to use this book:

1. Use this book to get your fundamentals cleared - Understand all the theoretical concepts involved in business communication and apply them practically.

2. Use the tips and strategies in the book to improve your business communication - Gain insights into how to skillfully communicate with your intended audience and draft written communication, proposals, reports, and presentations.

3. Learn from modern, relevant, and practical examples or case studies.

4. Understand the wrong approaches to business communication and eliminate them from your strategy.

5. Learn how to build an effective crisis communication strategy.

6. Test your knowledge with the multiple-choice quizzes provided at the end of every chapter.

So, you should use it as a dependable companion that you can regularly consult whenever you run into difficult business communication situations.

Who can benefit from this book?

Business Communication Essentials is for everyone who aspires to develop their business communication skills, whether you intend to learn how to write effective business reports, proposals, and presentations, or you are managing a team that requires that you use your business communication skills from time to time.

The following categories of readers will find this book to be of great help:

1. **Students:** If you are a university student pursuing a course in Business Studies, Business Administration, Business Management, Marketing, or any course that requires you to learn about business communication, you will unearth a wealth of information concerning business communication in this book.

2. **Teachers/Professors:** If you are a teacher/instructor of any business-related course, your students will gain a lot of insights from this book if you use it as your teaching material.

3. **Entrepreneurs/Business Owners/Executives/Managers/Supervisors:** Improve your business communication skills by digesting everything in this book and subsequently transform the way you communicate with the stakeholders associated with your business/organizations.

4. **Business/Management Researchers:** Discover some new approaches for doing business communication in this book.

5. **Managers/Administrators of Business Development Centers or Business Incubators:** This book will help you properly mentor the founders of businesses or startups you are incubating, developing, or investing in.

This page is intentionally left blank

Chapter 1

An Introduction to Business Communication

Business communication is an essential tool or channel for sharing important information among the stakeholders connected to a business or an organization. The stakeholders can be the organization's employees, managers, executives, suppliers, clients or customers, investors, and governmental agencies whose actions and/or decisions may affect the day-to-day running of the business.

It is imperative for an organization to design and implement a functional business communication strategy in order to fully encourage active participation of all its stakeholders in matters that will lead to higher productivity, improved performance, better decision-making, and faster problem-solving capability within and outside the organization.

The key learning objectives of this chapter should include the reader's understanding of the following:

- The definition of business communication

- The objectives of business communication

- Important concepts related to business communication

- Types of business communication

- Establishing credibility and incorporating fairness in business communication

1.1 What is Business Communication?

Business communication can simply be defined as the process of sharing vital business information among stakeholders within and outside an organization. To achieve its organizational goals and objectives, the management of an organization must engage in ongoing, efficient communication with its employees, who are its internal stakeholders. It is also important for employees and those who manage the organization's business activities to regularly reach out to its external stakeholders, such as the organization's clients/customers, suppliers, investors, partners, and governmental agencies.

For an organization to achieve efficient business communication, it must utilize both the traditional and modern communication tools at its disposal. We are living in a world where the patterns and styles of business communication are fast-changing, from face-to-face conversations to social, digital, and mobile interactions. Nowadays, emphasis is placed on collaborative business communication, which may entail that periodic one-on-one meetings are organized, online conference calls are carried out, and/or written messages are frequently exchanged among stakeholders.

Business communication is similar to personal communication in a number of ways. When a person demonstrates great communication skills, they can enjoy robust relationships, get a well-paying job, become an effective leader, and achieve significant success in their calling or profession. In comparison, any organization that fails to live up to modern business communication expectations would surely fall behind its competitors in the face of rising challenges to keep up with the vast, culturally diverse global marketplace.[1]

1.2 Why is Business Communication Important?

On a personal level, communication is necessary for directing, connecting, requesting for services, appreciating good gestures, and rewarding loyalists or supporters. The use of communication in business is pretty much the same; organizations employ the power of business communication to streamline their processes to achieve their organizational goals as scheduled.

On the other hand, the lack of efficient interdepartmental and interpersonal communication could cause an organization to lose focus while spending most of its time and scarce resources on solving both internal and external disagreements or problems,

---

1. Boyes, C. (2010). Communication (Collins Business Secrets). London: HyperCollins, p. 45.

instead of utilizing them for better performance and growth. Such an organization could be considered to be in a chaotic situation whereby the prevailing atmosphere does not support creativity, productivity, and advancement.

Some of the objectives organizations can achieve by implementing productive communication strategies include but are not limited to the following:

- **Quick and regular exchange of information:** Organizations thrive on the prompt and fast exchange of information among their stakeholders. For instance, the employees need regular and useful instructions from their managers to be able to successfully carry out their routine functions. Similarly, customers and clients of an organization need to be periodically updated about the organization's services and products as well as providing useful feedback that the organization could use in refining its products/services.

- **Motivating employees:** A good relationship ensues when there is robust and understandable communication between employees and their employers. This helps to improve their job satisfaction and streamline their education/training. It is also necessary for managers to direct their subordinates in the right direction.

- **Improving customer service:** When an organization implements a functional business communication strategy, it will be able to attract and retain loyal customers. It is through a well-structured communication process that clients/customers can obtain adequate information about a business and its products/services.

- **Facilitating business operations:** No organization can run on silence or poor communication procedures; employees require well-detailed information to understand the right things to do within the organization. In the same approach, external stakeholders need to be carried along to ensure that the organization has all the necessary requirements to operate smoothly and progress. For example, its suppliers should be informed about the possible supplies or raw materials and their corresponding quantities that the organization would utilize to run its operations. The local governmental agencies need to be updated about the organization's business activities so that it can obtain all the mandatory licenses and permissions and avoid operating illegally. All these processes could only be achieved through effective business communication.

- **Image or reputation management:** Organizational branding will not happen if an organization doesn't have great stories to tell about its missions/visions and products/services. This is because good storytelling can only be made with effective business communication.

- **Organizational goals:** When all the processes within and outside an organization are properly aligned through a well-executed business communication strategy, it will be easy for such an organization to achieve its goals and objectives.

- **Performance enhancement:** In a situation where an organization is falling behind in attaining all or some of its business goals, it takes efficient business communication to bring everything under control and enhance performance.

1.3 Important Concepts Related to Business Communication

Some of the important concepts concerning business communication are simply explained below. They are discussed in detail in different sections of this book.

1.3.1 Terms related to business communication

- **Sender:** As its name implies, a sender of communication is the person, organization, or group that initiates the communication. It must be emphasized that the sender is solely responsible for the success of the communication utilizing all the communication tools or resources at its disposal. As a sender, an organization can send a catalog of its new products to its customers.

- **Receiver:** On the other hand, a communication receiver is at the end of the communication spectrum, getting the messages or information initiated by the sender. In the example above, the customers are the receivers.

- **Channels of communication:** Business communication can be horizontal, lateral, or vertical depending primarily on the sender-receiver relationship and the communication's purpose, nature, flow, and intent.

  Horizontal communication refers to the communication between or among departments that are not on the same departmental level. Hence, there is no apparent competition between them, and they could collaborate on innovative projects by sharing vital information with one another.

On the contrary, *lateral communication* exists between departments on the same hierarchical level within an organization. The information shared between them may be necessary for collaboration and problem-solving since the departments would always interfere in one another's affairs due to the fact they may be working on the same project at the same time. *Vertical communication* occurs between employees at the lower ranks and their superiors (mostly managers and executives) who are at the upper end of the corporate ladder. Vertical communication could happen both ways, either as upward (bottom-up) communication or downward (top-down) communication. When lower-ranked employees send messages to their bosses, they are engaging in upward communication. On the other hand, when memos are issued by the directors or CEOs of organizations to their employees, it is a typical example of downward communication.

1.3.2 Methods of business communication

There are two main approaches or methods of business communication–verbal and non-verbal. *Verbal communication* relies on words to convey messages or share information with others. However, *non-verbal communication* utilizes body language, facial expressions, gestures, appearance, eye contact, and physical touches to send information to the receivers.

More information about these two methods of communication is provided in Chapter 9 of this book.

1.3.3 Methods of business communication

Communication could take place between the sender and the receiver via oral/verbal, non-verbal, written, electronic, or visual modes (see Figure 1.1).

Figure 1.1   Modes of business communication

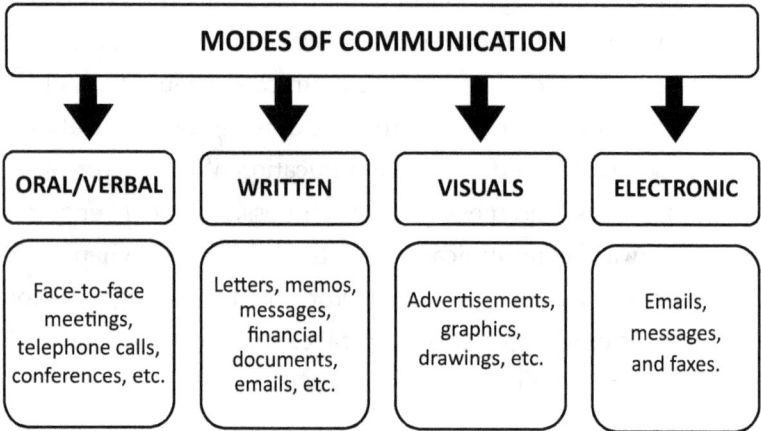

```
┌─────────────────────────────────────────────────────┐
│              MODES OF COMMUNICATION                   │
└─────────────────────────────────────────────────────┘
     ↓            ↓              ↓              ↓

┌────────────┐ ┌──────────┐ ┌──────────┐ ┌────────────┐
│ORAL/VERBAL │ │ WRITTEN  │ │ VISUALS  │ │ ELECTRONIC │
└────────────┘ └──────────┘ └──────────┘ └────────────┘

┌────────────┐ ┌──────────┐ ┌──────────┐ ┌────────────┐
│Face-to-face│ │Letters,  │ │Advertise-│ │Emails,     │
│meetings,   │ │memos,    │ │ments,    │ │messages,   │
│telephone   │ │messages, │ │graphics, │ │and faxes.  │
│calls,      │ │financial │ │drawings, │ │            │
│conferences,│ │documents,│ │etc.      │ │            │
│etc.        │ │emails,   │ │          │ │            │
│            │ │etc.      │ │          │ │            │
└────────────┘ └──────────┘ └──────────┘ └────────────┘
```

1.4 Types of Business Communication

In practice, there are two broad types of business communication—internal and external business communication. An organization needs to maintain a high level of efficiency in both its internal and external communication processes to position itself for unprecedented growth and subsequently outperform its rivals.

1.4.1 Internal communication

Intrinsically, there are two layers of internal communication—the communication between an **employer and his/her employees**, and the communication among **employees** within the same organization.

a. Employer-to-employee communication

In a small company of 5-10 employees, it is possible for their employer to communicate with them easily and regularly, whether by holding daily meetings or arranging weekly discussions with them. On the other, the situation becomes more complicated in an organization having one hundred or more employees. Whether the employer is the company's founder/CEO or a senior manager, the purpose of maintaining a culture of active communication with employees is to encourage unwavering commitment to the initial missions and visions of the company. People (workers) can go astray if they are not regularly reminded of their responsibilities within an organization. Therefore, it is not rare to see founders, executives, or managers of small and medium companies organizing daily, weekly, or monthly scheduled meetings with their employees. This is done to make sure that everyone is on the same page as far as actualizing the goals of the company.

b. Employee-to-employee communication

Since they are the engines that power their companies' business operations, it is crucial that employees are always kept in the loop. Whether they are working in offices or on the production/manufacturing lines, employees deserve to be updated from time to time. Think of it this way: It doesn't matter how well-equipped a company is, it will still be filled with unmotivated, redundant workers if they are not told exactly what to do. This is why employee-to-employee communication is essential. Unfortunately, employee communication in many companies is broken, and this problem often leaves workers in a difficult situation.

A report by McKinsey claimed that if organizations actively engage their employees through social interactions via some social technologies, they can be able to increase their workers' productivity by 20-25%.[2] This may involve creating a conducive social environment where workers can freely interact with one another, strengthening their relationships in the process and encouraging one another to do their best as far as their work (which they share together) is concerned.

Generally, the three main problems associated with employee communication are:

a. **Inaccessibility:** Some companies invest a lot of their resources in setting up communication assets such as an intranet, internal newsletters, mobile intranet app, employee surveys, collaboration tools, instant messaging tools, community channels, and so on. Unfortunately, not all employees know exactly how to use them; they either haven't received any training about the usability of the communication assets, or they have somehow forgotten how to utilize them. As expected, this supposedly break in the cycle of internal communication can disrupt the circulation of information within a company and lower its productivity.

b. **Little or no personalization:** When communication tools are personalized, they offer users more accessibility in

---

2. Chui, M. et al. (2012, July 1). The Social economy: Unlocking value and productivity through social technology. *McKinsey Global Institute.* https://www.mckinsey.com
www.vibrantpublishers.com

terms of deriving many benefits from using them. For example, a company may choose to personalize its intranet by streamlining its navigation tools and incorporating multilingual features in the system if the company deals with customers across many countries and cultures. More so, everything done on the intranet should be centered on the unique goals that the company aims to achieve. In this case, it is imperative the intranet be segmented into different teams or departments within the company, matching them only with the objectives they are working on.

c. **Comprehensive information:** It is one thing to set up effective employee communication systems, it is another to properly utilize them in transmitting comprehensive information to those (the employees) who mostly need them within the company. So, information should be timely and regularly communicated to the segments or sections of the employees who need to promptly act on it. Therefore, it is not just about passing inadequate information from one department of the company to the other, the communication must be detail-oriented, concise, clear, and comprehensive.

1.4.2 External communication

This is the process of communicating or interacting with people, corporate entities, and other stakeholders outside your company/organization. These outsiders may include suppliers, partners, customers, other businesses, investors, government agencies, and, of course, law enforcement.

As indicated above, an organization needs to carry the outsiders along so as to remain active in business. In other words, a company needs its customers, suppliers, investors, and partners to stay in business. Likewise, government agencies and law enforcement must be regularly updated to ensure that the company isn't operating illegally to avoid being shut down unexpectedly by the authorities. Hence, it takes good business communication to keep every stakeholder updated about the company's activities.

Some of the vital messages an organization may want to pass across to its external stakeholders include but are not limited to information about:

a. **Product development**

b. **Brand identity**

c. **Company news and achievements**

d. **Promotions, giveaways, and discounts**

e. **Financial releases**

f. **New service announcements**

Any or all of this information could be communicated to people externally via press releases, email, social media, phone, brochures, blog posts, white papers, live chat, periodic reports, and so on.

External business communication can be formal or informal, depending on the level of relationship with the audience. When contacting government agencies and law enforcement, an organization should use formal language. However, the tone could be informal or semi-formal when communicating with partners, suppliers, and existing customers.

1.5 Establishing Credibility and Incorporating Fairness In Business Communication

Unlike interpersonal communication, business communication is more structured, credible, and direct. If it is not done properly, it could have some negative effects on a company's reputation/brand identity as well as on its products/services.

Highlighted below are five strategic approaches an organization can adopt in making sure that all its communication with both internal and external stakeholders is perpetually credible:

a. **Honesty/Sincerity:** An organization/company can win the respect and trust of its employees, customers, suppliers, investors, and that of other people connected to it if its communication is usually honest or sincere. It is quite impracticable to run a company on lies; it is understandable that an organization that deceptively promotes its products/services to current and prospective customers will lose its credibility when the hidden falsehoods in its advertisements are discovered and exposed to the public. More so, even the organization's employees will lose trust in its crop of management. When this happens, it may be difficult to increase their morale and encourage them to do their best to promote the organization's interest.

b. **Objectiveness:** To be credible, business communication should be objective, direct, and detail-oriented. It should be perceived as an important exchange of information that is quite accurate and useful to the targeted audience. Otherwise, it may be considered insufficient and lacking impact. Many past employees of dubious organizations have been arrested and/or indicted due to the fact that they were previously working for a criminal organization that had defrauded people through falsehoods.

c. **Factuality:** Effective business communication is usually factual, conveying certain essential knowledge and facts. Take for instance, a company's press release or product catalog may be seen as useless and unhelpful if it doesn't contain the actual facts and exact information that the readers had expected to discover in it.

d. **Flawless delivery:** An organization should constantly work on achieving and maintaining flawless delivery of its communication messages. For instance, if a company promises its employees and customers a monthly newsletter, it must adhere to the promise. Failure to deliver as promised will cause the company to lose its credibility among its employees and customers.

e. **Understanding your audience:** The first thing an organization needs to do in order to flawlessly deliver its business information is to understand its targeted audience. Who are they? What kind of information do they regularly want? And how best to reach them?

The managers or executives of organizations should ensure that an environment for fairness in business communication is in place at their respective organizations. This entails that both the internal and external stakeholders related to the organizations must be given a fair amount of freedom to actively participate in whatever communication happening within the organization without any fear of sanction or censorship.[3]

---

3. Harvard Business School Press (2003). Business Communication (Harvard Business Essentials). New York: Harvard Business Review Press, p.25.

To create an environment that is genuinely welcoming to all manners of business communication, the following criteria must be considered:

a. **Openness:** A company should encourage openness as far as employer-to-employee and employee-to-employee communication is concerned. To achieve great business communication, employees shouldn't be afraid to speak their minds in front of their superiors. Similarly, the company should facilitate communication between its employees and external stakeholders. Great ideas are exchanged when people within an organization feel that their words won't be used against them in the end.

b. **Equitable opportunities:** A company should make it mandatory that people within the company are given equitable opportunities to express their opinions. In other words, some employees should not be allowed to talk endlessly during business meetings or deliberations while others are silenced.

c. **Flexibility:** Internal and external communication organized by an organization should be flexible enough so that the exchange of useful information is given more preference over being right. No new ideas could be generated by a company's employees if the management of the company operates with an inflexible pattern. Customers, on most occasions, admire interacting with flexible companies that can accommodate their needs at all times. Investors often include a "flexibility clause" when signing a contract with companies they are putting their financial resources in. Nothing is permanent; change is the only permanent thing. So, any company that fails to embrace flexibility cannot grow or progress in business.

d. Moral obligations: Everyone who is involved in business communication is bound by the moral obligations to initiate, share, choose, and process information that is beneficial to those involved in the communication for the sole benefit of the concerned company. Threats and messages of altercation have no place in constructive business communication. Each information exchanged is expected to be useful, pragmatic, and beneficial to the central organization.

e. Fair play: Great business communication emanates from a constant practice of honesty and impartiality. This entails that there must be fair-play rules of engagement among all stakeholders involved in the communication. More so, the decisions that often lead to the communication must be criteria-based—no one should be singled out for embarrassment for airing their opinions, as long as they are factual and good for the benefit of the organization they are all related to. Companies need to prevent unfair advantage from taking place among their employees. Everyone should have the unique opportunity to contribute meaningfully to the communication in the companies they are working for.

f. Human rights issues: Whether it happens in a business or outside of a company, employers should always recognize the fact that communication is everyone's fundamental human right. Article 19 of the Universal Declaration on Human Rights *"Everyone has the right to freedom of opinion and expression; this right includes freedom to hold opinions without interference and to seek, receive and impart information and ideas through any media and regardless of frontiers."* Organizations should make sure that their employees' human rights are duly protected. The same thing applies to customers, partners, investors, and others.

Quiz

1. **Business communication can be mainly divided into _____ separate types.**

   a. 4

   b. 2

   c. 5

2. **For business communication to be considered credible, it must be**

   a. Dishonest

   b. Factual

   c. Long

3. **All of these are external stakeholders to a company with the exception of**

   a. Team leader in the company

   b. Investors

   c. Customers

4. **Employer-to-employee business communication is an example of _____**

   a. Both internal and external communication

   b. Internal communication

   c. External communication

5. Business communication is vital because companies use it as a medium for connecting with internal and external stakeholders. True or false?

   a. False

   b. True

6. Law enforcement can be categorized as an _____

   a. Internal stakeholder

   b. External stakeholder

   c. Neither an internal nor an external stakeholder

7. Brand identity, advertisements, and press releases are examples of important information an organization may want to pass across to its external stakeholders. True or false?

   a. True

   b. False

8. When a project manager gives useful instructions to workers in his department, this is a typical example of _____

   a. Internal business communication

   b. External business communication

   c. Both internal and external business communication

9. **The employees of a company named Bigger Sports are complaining that they cannot access the necessary information on their company's communication. What should the company do to solve this problem?**

   a. Demote the workers

   b. Reduce their salaries

   c. Personalize the information on its websites and apps

10. **Which of these is not one of the objectives of business communication?**

   a. Winning a service award

   b. Brand/reputation management

   c. Great customer service

Answers	1 – b	2 – b	3 – a	4 – b	5 – b
	6 – b	7 – a	8 – a	9 – c	10 – a

Chapter Summary

◆ Business communication is of two main kinds: Internal and external business communication.

◆ Internal business communication occurs within a company or an organization. It is essentially the form of communication between an employer or executives of the company and the employees working for the company. It can also include communication among employees of the same company.

◆ External business communication occurs between the organization and people outside it. These people may include the organization's customers, investors, partners, government agencies, law enforcement, etc.

◆ For business communication to be recognized, it must exhibit some characteristics of credibility and fairness.

◆ Some of the objectives of business communication are for organizations to be able to achieve optimum productivity, motivate their employees, offer top-notch customer services to their clients/customers, and maintain a great, enviable reputation in the marketplace.

◆ The three main channels of business communication are vertical, lateral, and horizontal.

Chapter 2

Understanding Your Audience

Businesses/companies use communication to connect with their audiences. It is a fact that the quality of every business communication depends largely on how well the communicators (businesses, in this case) understand their audiences (employees, partners, investors, etc.). In the absence of mutual understanding between the communicators and their targeted audiences, whatever is being communicated will only remain in a vacuum and will become a source of confusion and misunderstanding. It is safe to say that the very first step in achieving effective and goal-oriented business communication is for companies to fully understand the nature of who they are trying to communicate with, that is, their audience.

The key learning objectives of this chapter should include the reader's understanding of the following:

- The tools required to understand your audiences, such as demographic traits and overall perceptions

- The strategies to analyze your audience, that is, the three types of audience analysis

2.1 Tools to Understand Your Audience

An organization's audience could be its employees, customers, partners, investors, suppliers, or governmental agencies. This chapter focuses on how an organization, through in-depth analyses, can practically identify its main audience–both internal and external audiences–with the hope of proactively communicating with them.

A company can derive much information about its audience by analyzing their demographic traits, perceptions, and behavioral patterns. The data obtained from these analyses could be used in providing better services or in manufacturing great products that the audience would like. Moreover, organizations can smoothly carry their employees along once it has discovered how best to communicate with those employees.

Without knowing who the audience is and how they would receive messages, an organization may find itself spending a lot on advertisement or internal communication but not making any tangible progress in its business communication initiatives.[4] Given below are a few tools that will help businesses understand their audiences.

2.1.1 Demographic traits

Not every message an organization or company puts out there will accomplish its purpose(s). One of the powerful reasons for ineffective business communication is not paying genuine attention to the demographic traits of your targeted audience. In essence, people tend to respond to what (messages, advertisements, etc.) tickles their fancy and speaks to their central needs. Take for example, if a person is looking for a body cream to cure the acne or pimples on their face, they probably won't be paying attention to any advertisements on tobacco. Failure to recognize that each audience belongs to a certain demographic can cost an organization a lot in poorly targeted advertisements or promotions as far as external communication is concerned.

Generally, audience demographics can be categorized under:

a. **Age:** People of different ages act differently; more so, they do not receive messages in the same way. Even if two people are looking for the same product, say a game, their choices would be quite different based on their ages and interests—while the older person might go for a creative and highly educational game such as Monopoly or Word Scramble, the younger individual might only be interested in action games like Zelda or Super Mario. This entails that businesses need to pay attention to age-specific

4. Robles, M.M. (2012). Executive Perceptions of the Top 10 Soft Skills Needed in Today's Workplace. *Business and Professional Communication Quarterly.* 75(4), p.460 doi:10.1177/1080569912460400

requirements when targeting potential customers with their business messages. Similarly, more experienced and elderly employees will process intra-company messages differently than younger employees, and therefore, internal business messages also require considering the age of the receiver.

b. **Geographic location:** Companies should realize that people residing in different locations will value business communication that specifically addresses the issues affecting their localities. For example, urban or city-dwellers are likely going to respond faster to a piece of information about how to protect themselves against cybercrimes than those who live in rural areas or villages who don't think that cybersecurity is an issue for them, or who don't even know what cybersecurity means.

c. **Ethnicity:** People are of various races; hence, organizations shouldn't overlook ethnic sensibilities when communicating with people from different ethnicities or races. Sometimes, organizations are compelled to change their names, logos, or their products' names to avoid being branded as racist. Some of the recent examples included Nestle changing its candies' names from Red Skins to Red Ripper and Chicos to Cheekies because both Red Skins and Chicose were offensive to people of the First Nations in North America and Latin America respectively.

d. **Gender:** People of different genders may respond to information differently. To make their messages understandable to their audience, companies are required to utilize inclusive and gender-specific terms and expressions.

e. **Level of education:** Companies should factor in the levels of education of their audience when communicating with them. This may influence the choice of language, the complexity of instructions or information, and the methods of delivering those business messages. It would be ineffective to use difficult vocabulary or difficult business jargon when sending an email to someone who only has a high school diploma and may not even understand what the message is all about. On the other hand, such messages might be easy for college graduates to understand. While communicating with customers it is always better to use simple language that all sections of society can understand.

f. **Household income level:** How much households have can determine their responsiveness to messages or advertisements from a company. Due to higher disposable incomes, the middle-class and upper-middle-class can respond favorably to information relating to expensive goods/services; low-class customers won't respond at all to prices that may break their banks.

g. **Marital status:** Single and married people see things differently. Hence, communicating with them in the same way will fail woefully.

h. **Occupation:** Organizations need to customize communication based on their targeted audience's jobs or occupations. The best approach to getting someone's attention is to give them news or information that would excite them. A medical doctor may have nothing to do with a combined harvester; but if such a machine is marketed to farmers, they will at least show some interest in it.

i. **Homeownership:** How do you expect someone who doesn't own a home to respond positively to companies selling home insurance? That's a typical example of poorly targeted business communication.

It is quite interesting to notice that each demographic exhibits traits that are similar in nature, and these characteristics guide their consumer habits and the way they respond to messages sent out by different companies. The fact is that communication is all about exchanging meaningful and helpful messages between one party and the other.

2.1.2 Overall perceptions

Perception in communication is referred to as the act of choosing, arranging, and interpreting information. This indicates that people, including ourselves, will only choose to interpret information that is considered to be of utmost significance to us. For example, when there's news about an impending snowstorm on cable television, like CNN, people living in tropical countries won't ever bother themselves with preparing for the snowstorm, because they have no winter that could bring snowstorms. Only people residing in cold countries will spend their time and resources making arrangements to protect themselves and their loved ones from the approaching snowstorm. The same logic applies to business communication.

Two-way perceptions

Perception, as an essential factor in business communication, is never a one-way thing. It is indeed a two-way experience. How your audience perceives you or your company will go a long way to determining if they will continue to listen to your messages (advertisements, product releases, etc.) and interpret them to their advantage.

| Figure 2.1 | The principle of two-way perception |

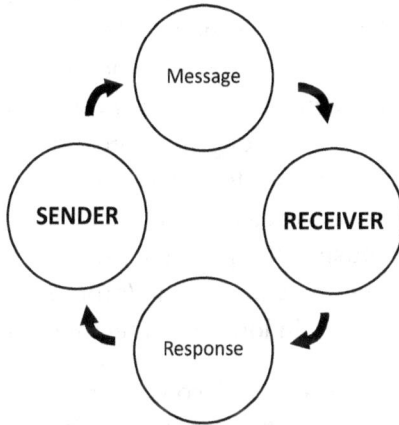

Figure 2.1 Demonstrates the principle of two-way perception. The sender (a business/an organization) releases the message to the receiver (its employees, customers, partners, investors, etc.). The receiver decodes or interprets the message and then offers an appropriate response.

So, both the sender's and receiver's perceptions are important in determining the success of any form of business communication. It is natural for external stakeholders to hold a certain idea about your products/services. Similarly, the way you perceive your audiences will influence the nature of the information you pass across to them. Are they physiologically, culturally, or emotionally attuned in a way that they can use their sensory, olfactory, tactile, auditory sense, or power of sight to decode the message you are sending to them?

Types of perceptions in communication

a. **Physiological perception:** Most of the information about the things we see, hear, feel, smell, or taste are sent to our brain where the interpretation of the information takes place. Even business communication, which can either be verbal or nonverbal, can be visualized in people's brains. In this case, they feel, sense, or experience a company's messages as if they were physical things, through visualizations. In order to make the strongest impression on your audience, you should concentrate on messages that offer more benefits to them or use words that will excite them. In the same approach, businesses are encouraged to utilize memorable visuals in their advertisements/promotions so that the images can remain longer on their audience's minds.

b. **Previous experiences:** A consumer's previous experiences with a business may affect the way they perceive the company. If their previous experiences were great, that business will have a loyal customer who will continue to patronize its products/services. On the other hand, if their past experiences were horrible, the business can even lose some or all of its customers in no time. Michael LeBoeuf, a former management professor at the University of New Orleans, said that "a satisfied customer is the best strategy of all." If you give your customers good experiences to cherish, they will in return support your business all the time.

c. **Cultural perception:** Every company by default has its own corporate culture—how they run their activities, including how they interact with customers, partners, and other external stakeholders. Everyone understands that Apple, Inc.'s culture is all about the design and useful functionality of its products. Each organization's culture can promote or hinder its communication with both its employees and external stakeholders. It is generally believed that a great company culture considers its employees' welfare. Corporate culture is also built into a company's products/

services and has some influence on the designs of the promotional materials used by the company. Partners and investors can easily relate to this culture and notice its priority in their communication with the company.

d. **Current feelings:** People's current feelings can seriously affect the type of information they will be willing to accept and process. If they have enjoyed great interactions with a company before, consumers will ecstatically jump at the new promotional messages from the company. In this way, investors will choose to invest in a business they have already had great relationships with, which is in their good books. It is safe to say that the happier people are about a business, the more satisfying communication they will have with that business or the representatives of the business.

Customer perception is one of the ways utilized by businesses to know what their customers are thinking about them and their products/services to better serve them. An organization can detect or learn about how its customers feel about it through any or all of the procedures highlighted below:

- **Periodic surveys:** Regularly providing customer satisfaction surveys to customers for them to describe how they feel about a business or an organization. Figure 2.2 is a sample of a customer satisfaction survey. It reveals the kinds of information a business may want to elicit from its customers through such surveys.

- **Social media eavesdropping:** Businesses can eavesdrop on their customer's comments and complaints while using the organization's official website to know what their pain points are and how to solve them. Organizations can learn a lot about their customers' behavioral patterns by placing polls within their official social media posts.

- **Organized market research:** Alternatively, an organization can commission a third party (for example, a market research agency) to help it comprehensively survey its customers.

Figure 2.2   **A sample of a customer satisfaction survey**

Customer Satisfaction Survey

Thank you for taking the Customer Satisfaction Survey. The Survey should take less than five minutes of your time to Click the "Submit by Email" button to submit the survey or "Print" the form and fax it to us.

1 = very satisfied   2 = somewhat satisfied   3 = neutral   4 = somewhat dissatisfied   5 = very dissatisfied

	1	2	3	4	5
1. How satisfied are you with with the delivery of our products?	O	O	O	O	O
2. How do you rate the response time of our Sales Representatives?	O	O	O	O	O
3. How satisfied are you with the quality of our products?	O	O	O	O	O
4. How satisfied are you with the quality of our Custom Gasketing Products?	O	O	O	O	O
5. How do you rate our customer communications?	O	O	O	O	O
6. How would you rate the PRODUCT KNOWLEDGE of our:					
a) Order Desk/Inside Sales Representatives	O	O	O	O	O
b) Outside Sales Representatives	O	O	O	O	O
c) Counter/Showroom Sales Representatives	O	O	O	O	O
7. Rate your overall satisfaction with the customer service.	O	O	O	O	O

8. What product and/or service characteristics do you like?

9. What product and/or service characteristics do you dislike?

Source: print.hpeasystart.com

It must be stated that the above-mentioned approaches can also be applied to unravel employee perception, investor perception, and other stakeholder perceptions as well.

2.2 Strategies for Analyzing Your Audience

After knowing their audience's demographic characteristics and perceptions, companies can use the following analytic strategies to tailor their communication according to their target audience. Answering the following questions will help businesses create compelling messages that will appeal to their intended audience.[5]

1. Situational analysis: Before communicating with your audience, know what situations they are in. What kind of environment do they live in? What choice of words or messages will resonate with them? For example, if your customer survey or social media eavesdropping reveals that your customer is struggling with how to use one of your company's products, it is wrong to market another product to him or her. The right thing to do is to first take the time to explain how the customer can happily use the product they have already purchased. Once the customer is satisfied with your first product, they will be willing to try out your other products. In the same way, you don't send a message that is meant for a government agency to a supplier. Every act of communication must have a purpose, and its audience must be in the most appropriate situation to receive it.

---

5. Tuff, A. (2015, June 19). 10 Ways to Create a Culture of Open Communication. *Columbia Business*. Retrieved from https://leading.business.columbia.edu

2. **Psychological analysis:** The primary goal of a psychological analysis is to get into the head of your audience. What are they thinking before or after communicating with them? What are their beliefs about you and your products/ services? How do their beliefs align with your company's visions/missions? Will they be able to change their minds after you communicate with them? A company can send out surveys to both its customers and suppliers to find out exactly what they think about its products/services. The surveys may reveal some information about the perception of the company. The good thing is that this information may be used in communicating with them to effect positive actions or increase their loyalty to the company.

3. **Topic interest and prior knowledge analysis:** Effective communication occurs when you tell people or organizations exactly what they are interested in hearing from you. It is even more satisfying when your audience already has some knowledge about the subject matter that you want to discuss with them. It speeds up the communication process and leaves you and your audience in a better place having smoothly exchanged information or ideas that may be beneficial to both of you. Analyzing your audience demographics and customer surveys to understand how much prior knowledge they have will help you tailor your communication effectively.

Quiz

1. **Why is it important for organizations to fully understand their audiences in business communication?**

   a. To know who to send what business messages to

   b. To stop selling products to them

   c. To invite them to the organization's get-together lunch

2. **Businesses use communication to connect with their customers, investors, and partners. True or false?**

   a. False

   b. True

3. **What is the best way to define demographic traits?**

   a. They are the similar characteristics exhibited by some people in the same place, of the same age or gender.

   b. It is a method for detecting customers' satisfaction through surveys.

   c. It is the ability to communicate with body language.

4. **Which of these is not one of the proper ways of creating a fair environment for business communication?**

   a. Being partial

   b. Being open

   c. Being flexible

5. Communication, in business as well as generally in life, is regarded as one of the basic human rights. True or false?

   a. True.

   b. False.

6. What does "physiological perception" mean in business communication?

   a. It is human's ability to perceive things as we see, hear, feel, smell, or taste them.

   b. It means seeing things through the eyes of one's culture.

   c. It is a marketing tactic.

7. Which of these doesn't fall under "occupation" as an example of demographic traits?

   a. Male/Female

   b. Entrepreneur

   c. Firefighter

8. How can organizations use their knowledge from "situational analysis" to target new customers?

   a. Conducting a situational analysis is unnecessary.

   b. They can engage in business communication with new customers by sending messages that specifically address their current situations.

   c. There is no way organizations can use their knowledge from situational analysis.

9. Which of these two companies creates the fairer atmosphere for business communication among its employees? Company T gives its employees equal opportunity to communicate with one another; Company S doesn't allow fair play in communication among its employees.

   a. Company S.

   b. Company T.

10. When an investor wants to put their money into a business, one of the factors for consideration is the business's "corporate culture". In business communication, this is referred to as _____

    a. physiological perception

    b. cultural perception

    c. demographic perception

Answers	1 – a	2 – b	3 – a	4 – a	5 – a
	6 – a	7 – a	8 – b	9 – b	10 – b

Chapter Summary

◆ The first step in achieving effective business communication is to know the nature of the audience that will be targeted with some messages.

◆ Demographic traits of an audience reveal a lot about their age, gender, location, ethnicity, culture, religious affiliation, occupation, family size, marital status, etc.

◆ There are four unique audience analyses: demographic analysis, situational analysis, psychological, topic interest, and previous knowledge analysis.

◆ In business communication, both the communicator and the audience hold different perceptions of each other, and it is imperative that they know which perceptions they have about each other.

◆ Organizations should create a comfortable environment for fairness in communication with their internal and external stakeholders.

◆ Organizations can obtain a wealth of information/ data about their customers. employees, investors, etc. by undertaking customer, employee, or investor perception analysis.

Chapter 3

How to Achieve Great Interpersonal Communication

Rollo May, a well-known American humanistic psychologist, reportedly said that *"communication leads to community, that is, to understanding intimacy and mutual valuing."* This statement supports the fact that if our communication is great, we can create a community or team of excited people who respectfully exchange values and intimately connect with one another. Therefore, good interpersonal communication is required to bring people together around a cause or a purpose with the view of achieving a common goal. This purpose may be to maintain quality in a business's/company's products/services or to increase the overall production levels.

> The key learning objectives of this chapter should include the reader's understanding of the following:
>
> - The effects of emotional intelligence on interpersonal communication
>
> - Team building and communication
>
> - Global communication

3.1 Interpersonal Communication Defined

Interpersonal communication can be defined as an exchange of information between two or more people. There has been some research on how human beings use verbal communication (with words) and nonverbal communication (with body language and facial expressions) to form, sustain, and deepen interpersonal relationships. Figure 3.1 is a visual representation of interpersonal communication.[6]

There are four distinct types of interpersonal communication in every organization:

- **Oral communication or Verbal:** This is also known as "spoken" communication, and it involves discussing in person or one-on-one with people within an organization using words. Oral communication is explained in detail in Chapter 4.

- **Nonverbal communication:** This kind of communication doesn't necessarily require words. However, the

---

communicators can use body language, gestures, or facial expressions to pass information across to one another.

- **Written communication:** As its name implies, this form of business communication entails using the written format, such as email, business proposals, catalogs, memos, etc. to pass important information within an organization, as well as using it to interact with its external stakeholders. Detailed descriptions of written communication and its uses in business are provided in other chapters of this book.

- **Listening:** Not until recently, communication experts don't inevitably consider listening as a form of communication. However, it is now classified as a communication type, since good listening skill is regarded as an important soft skill everyone working within a team should possess.

Figure 3.1 **Interpersonal Communication**

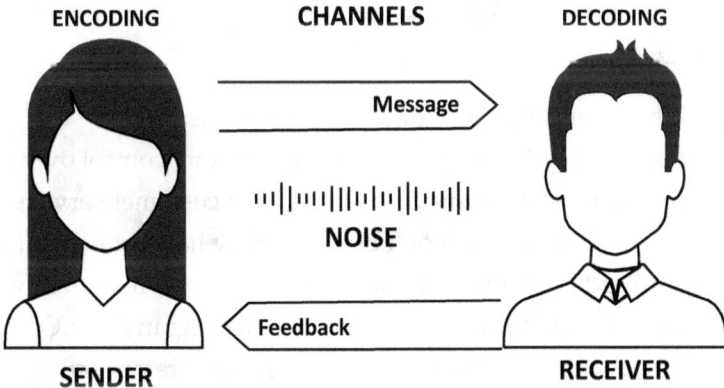

ENCODING	CHANNELS	DECODING
	Message	
	NOISE	
	Feedback	
SENDER		**RECEIVER**

3.2 The Effects of Emotional Intelligence on Interpersonal Communication

Simply defined, Emotional Intelligence (EI) or Emotional Quotient (EQ) is the ability of a person to manage, utilize, and control his/her emotions in a positive way that will produce empathy towards others. Empathy refers to the practice of understanding other people's feelings sympathetically; it could also mean having the ability to feel what others are feeling. As a business owner, you are expected to empathize with your customers when they are having trouble enjoying your products/ services.

Over the years, communication experts have linked emotional intelligence with great business communication. It is believed that someone with high emotional intelligence, be it a company's CEO, manager, customer service representative, or team leader, often demonstrates enviable and great communication skills. As a matter of fact, a high emotional quotient can turn you into someone:

a. **Who has firm control of his/her emotions:** A high emotional quotient (EQ) will give you more control over your emotions. In this case, if you are a customer service representative, you won't be angered by harsh statements from rude customers. In the same way, you will patiently discuss with partners or investors as a company's CEO, even though you are well aware that they are not acting in the interest of your business. Being able to rein in one's emotions is a great skill many business managers don't have. Interestingly, they all need this important skill to be able to communicate clearly and decisively with other stakeholders.

b. **Who is a confident, persuasive speaker or negotiator:**
   High emotional intelligence transforms you into a natural, confident, and persuasive speaker or negotiator. Having systematically removed overbearing emotions from your negotiations, you will be able to convince others with facts and carefully chosen words. Have you ever heard of any hot-headed company's CEO who often picked fights with his/her employees and disrespected his/her company's external stakeholders but still did well in business? It is very rare! Business owners and their employees need high emotional intelligence to hold meaningful business communication.

c. **Who can genuinely influence other people:** When you have exceedingly improved in controlling your emotions and communicating clearly with facts and confidence, your audience will trust you. In this case, they will believe whatever you say, and this could give you leverage to genuinely influence them. One of the main reasons business communication fails is that those involved in the process allow self-interests to overtake objective reasoning or logic. However, when you can put your emotions in check and abhor self-centeredness, your audience will gladly accept your statements or submissions on any issues.

3.3 Team Building and Communication

For a well-aligned team to be built, streamlined communication is required. As shown in Figure 3.2, the sender must encode the message he thinks the receiver will be able to decode easily, with little to no confusion or misunderstanding. When quality messages or instructions are released from the point of origin, they will be accepted, interpreted, and utilized to achieve their intended purpose at the point of receipt.

In practice, what matters, nowadays, is the quality of the communication, not necessarily the distance between the sender and the receiver. This section of the book looks at some important factors for building a resilient, effective team based on the regular exchange of quality communication among all the team members.

Figure 3.2   Elements of Interpersonal Communication

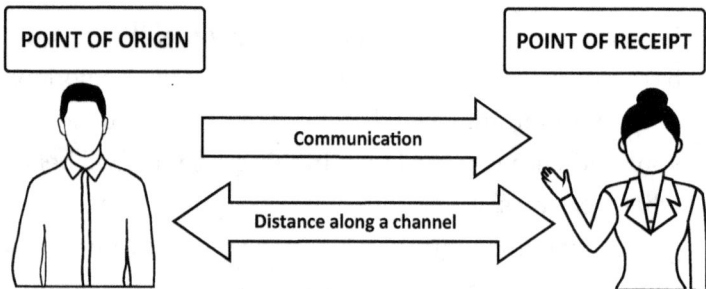

One of the most thoughtful quotes about team building is attributed to Patrick Lencioni, the famous author of *"The Five Dysfunctions of A Team,"* and it reads thus: *"Teamwork requires some sacrifice up front, people who work as a team have to put the collective needs of the group ahead of their individual interests."* That is the best description of team building! While building a team within an organization, it is natural to presume that it will involve a lot of communication. However, the nature of business communication that can strengthen any team must meet the following expectations from all members of the team:

a. **Reliability:** The employer, manager, or even team supervisor must be reliable for everyone within an organization to take his/her words seriously. In the same way, a sales representative discussing a company's product/ service must appear dependable to customers before they can purchase such a product or subscribe to the service the sales representative is busy marketing. It is not enough to give wonderful promises or assurances to members of a team, the manager or company's CEO must back them up with actions to be considered reliable.

b. **Being considerate:** Every member of a team is expected to sacrifice their time, skills, and other required resources to keep the team together. However, the communication among a team must be truly considerate—this entails that no one pursues self-interest and causes disaffection among team members. More so, words that reflect mutual respect and understanding must be used from time to time.

c. **Clarity/No ambiguity:** Clarity of communication is what keeps team members together on most occasions. Team managers and leaders are expected to provide instructions that are clear and understandable. The conversations among team members should be less ambiguous to erase any instances of misunderstanding.

d. **Communal benefits:** The communication utilized by team leaders and members should express communal benefits. In other words, efforts should be deployed toward using expressions that edify the company. Therefore, instead of using self-centered statements like "I did this; I did that", this could be changed to "We did this; we did that"! If the team should feel recognized and their efforts valued, it should be done at the community level, because a team is actually a community within an organization.

e. **Significance:** The communication among team members must be of significant value to their assigned roles within the team so that each member can derive some form of motivation from it. This indicates that worthless arguments and unedifying words should not be used in team-building communication. Team members will consider any information that they can utilize in developing their skills and adapt to better carry out their respective duties within the team and, of course, at the company. Gossip or backbiting are examples of insignificant communication that must be avoided at all costs. Instead, actionable instructions and discussions should replace conversations that often lead to avoidable arguments and quarrels within the organization.

3.4 Global Communication

Nowadays, not only multinational companies engage in global communication, but also a small startup located anywhere around the globe can begin attending to a slew of international customers/clients right from its launch day. The internet, as we know, has turned the entire world into a global village and we are connected at the click of our computer mouse.

So, what is global communication? Global or international communication can be defined as the development and exchange of information, which can be through verbal and nonverbal messages, designed mainly for international audiences such as cross-continental clients/customers.

Assuming a new startup named XYZ located in New Delhi wants to market its Software as a Service (SaaS) products to potential clients/customers around the world, the founder of the startup or its managing executives must position the small company towards global communication.

Then, how can XYZ implement effective international/global communication? The answer to this cogent question is not far-fetched: XYZ can follow these three modalities for achieving powerful global communication:

a. **Embrace diversity:** Hiring and training employees from different races, cultures, religious, and political affiliations can boost XYZ's plan to go global from the day it was launched. Its diverse team, when properly trained, can utilize its ethnic and cultural resources to help XYZ reach prospective clients/customers across various cultures and races.[7]

b. **Globalize its messages:** XYZ needs to set up a small, in-house media department that is focused on delivering global messages to people in the targeted locations.

c. **Customize site navigation:** It is also important to make sure that people residing in the countries targeted by XYZ can smoothly navigate its website. This can be accomplished by customizing its site navigations.

Globalization has come to stay, and it is only companies that plan, implement, and maintain global or international communication that can win the race.

---

7. Hynes, G.E. (2012). Improving employees' interpersonal communication competencies: A qualitative study. *Business and Professional Communication Quarterly,* 75(4), p. 472. https://doi.org/10.1177/1080569912458965

Quiz

1. Effective business communication, according to Rollo May, can lead to a community. True or false?

   a. True

   b. False

2. Sharing information between two or more people is referred to as _____

   a. Interpersonal communication

   b. Global communication

   c. Emotional intelligence

3. People with high emotional intelligence can engage in good communication. True or false?

   a. False

   b. True

4. What is "emotional intelligence"?

   a. It is the process of getting new customers.

   b. It is the ability of human beings to feel what other people are feeling.

   c. It is a type of consumer product.

5. **"Emotional intelligence" is also known as** _____

   a. Emotional Quotient (EQ)

   b. Ability

   c. Five senses

6. **Which of the approaches is not required for a company to do well in its global communication efforts?**

   a. Globalizing its messages

   b. Embracing diversity

   c. Buying global advertisements

7. **In today's world, businesses can start selling their products around the world from their launch day. True or false?**

   a. True

   b. False

8. **Multinational companies rely mainly on global business communication to win more international clients. True or false?**

   a. False

   b. True

9. **Great teams are built on communication that is basically**

   _____

   a. Reliable

   b. Dishonest

   c. Partial

10. **What does this expression mean? Team members are usually advised to use communication that reveals "communal benefits".**

   a. It means that individual achievements shouldn't be celebrated above communal achievements.

   b. It means companies can spend their money to establish communities.

   c. It means team members' opinions don't matter at all.

Answers	1 – a	2 – a	3 – b	4 – b	5 – a
	6 – c	7 – a	8 – b	9 – a	10 – a

Chapter Summary

◆ It is believed that people with high emotional intelligence or emotional quotient can achieve good interpersonal communication.

◆ Great business communication is required to build wonderful teams in companies.

◆ Global or international communication is all about producing messages with a global context to reach audiences in some targeted locations around the world.

◆ Embracing diversity is one of the surest ways for a company to do well in global communication.

This page is intentionally left blank

Chapter 4

Oral Communication

For centuries, oral communication has been used as the medium of genuinely connecting with people. Teachers pass instructions to their students using oral communication. In the same way, parents employ it to guide their children in the right direction in life. Businesses are not particularly left behind in the usage of oral communication; an employer can hold intimate and meaningful meetings with his/her employees using the same oral communication.

Over the past decades, communication experts have duly investigated how the usefulness of this important communication tool can be expanded for all manners of business communication. Some outcomes of their research efforts are discussed in this chapter.

The key learning objectives of this chapter should include the reader's understanding of the following:

- Types of oral communication

- Understanding your different listeners

- The 7 Cs of oral communication

4.1 Oral Communication and Its Types

Figure 4.1 describes the oral communication process, how the message moves from the sender to the receiver, highlighting the importance of encoding and decoding the sent messages while eliminating noises during oral communication.

Figure 4.1   **The Oral Communication Process**

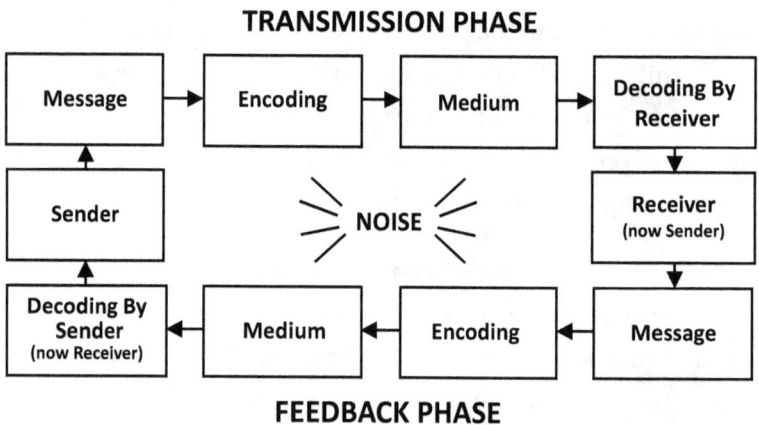

TRANSMISSION PHASE

| Message | → | Encoding | → | Medium | → | Decoding By Receiver |

| Sender | | NOISE | | Receiver (now Sender) |

| Decoding By Sender (now Receiver) | ← | Medium | ← | Encoding | ← | Message |

FEEDBACK PHASE

Adapted from: oralcom.wordpress.com [8]

Communication is divided into three main forms: verbal, non-verbal, and written communication. Oral communication is a

8. "The Process of Communication." ORAL COMMUNICATION IN CONTEXT, October 14, 2016. https://oralcom.wordpress.com.

form of verbal communication.[9]

One common example of oral communication theory describes the practice as an act of interaction and correction. This is very true in the sense that an employer can utilize oral communication to pass vital business information across to his/her employees and use the same tool to chastise them when they do something wrong.

Broadly speaking, oral communication is divided into three distinct types:

a. **Face-to-face communication:** Communication experts continue to believe that face-to-face communication is the best and the most effective way of personally connecting with others and building enduring trust. In the age of email and social media, we seem to have quickly forgotten that one-on-one conversations lead to robust and dependable relationships. In a company setting, team leaders or project managers can have great close discussions with their subordinates by looking eye-to-eye with them. In families, parents emphasize talking directly to their children if they do anything wrong because they naturally believe that their words carry more weight in person than by writing angry messages or making a phone call. The same philosophy is applicable in business communication. People (investors, customers, partners, suppliers, etc.) can misinterpret the contents of emails or letters, but when they engage with a company's CEO face-to-face, such misunderstanding could be quickly laid to rest or resolved.

---

9. Binnion, J.E., and Thomas, E.G. (1977). A Course in Oral Communication in Business. *Business and Professional Communication Quarterly*, 40(1), p. 12-5. https://eric.ed.gov

Even though face-to-face communication is a kind of oral communication, it is possible for those who are engaged in it to simultaneously pick up some nonverbal cues such as facial expressions, sign language, and body language.

b. **Telephone conversations:** Telephone conversation is the second most popular type of oral communication. From using old landline telephones to modern-day cell phones and smartphones, a great percentage of business communication now takes place through phone conversations. The wide application of smartphones and cell phones has drastically reduced the cost of making a phone call and gives users more freedom to reach anyone they want at any time.

c. **Meeting discussions:** Small businesses have an average of 2-10 meetings per week depending on their sizes and the number of participants or their employees in these meetings. Nowadays meetings can be conducted physically or virtually. In recent years, the coronavirus pandemic (COVID-19) has increased the number of virtual or online business meetings across the globe. Companies use meetings to discuss vital information about their day-to-day operations or to introduce newer or more improved ways of running their business activities.

4.2 Understanding Your Different Listeners

In reality, there are 4 types of listeners as shown in Figure 4.2. These are active, passive, evaluative listeners, and non-listeners.

Figure 4.2 **Types of Listeners**

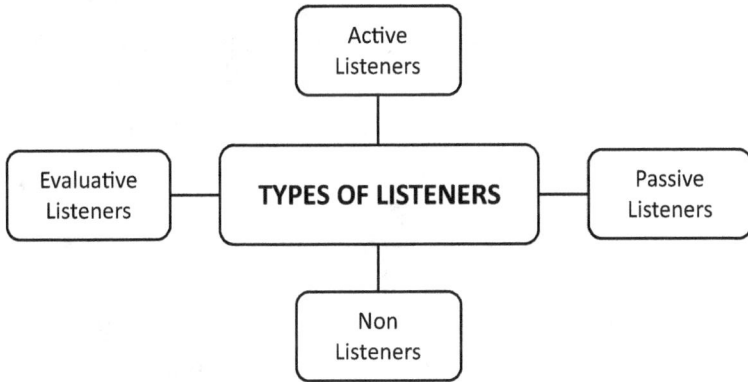

```
                    ┌─────────────┐
                    │   Active    │
                    │  Listeners  │
                    └──────┬──────┘
                           │
┌─────────────┐   ┌────────┴────────┐   ┌─────────────┐
│ Evaluative  │───│ TYPES OF LISTENERS │───│   Passive   │
│  Listeners  │   │                 │   │  Listeners  │
└─────────────┘   └────────┬────────┘   └─────────────┘
                           │
                    ┌──────┴──────┐
                    │     Non     │
                    │  Listeners  │
                    └─────────────┘
```

Active listeners proactively pay attention to whatever you may be saying. On the other hand, passive listeners are not concentrating on the information you are trying to pass across to them; they take in only 15-20% of the information being said. Evaluative listeners may be active or passive listeners, but they are only listening to obtain some concrete facts about the matter under discussion; they are not there to be entertained. Non-listeners aren't listening at all–they are the worst kind of listeners to have in a communication loop.

4.3 Active Listening

Of all the four types of listening, there is only one type of listening that moves a conversation forward: Active listening. As was mentioned, this is the listening that is proactively paying attention to what is being said. This type of listening is done with the intention to capture the meaning of what message is being conveyed by the person speaking. Zeno of Citium stated, *"We have two ears and one mouth, so we should listen more than we say."* Stephen Covey, in his book, Seven Habits of Highly Effective People exhorted us with the statement, *"Seek first understanding, then be understood,"* which implies that we, as party to a conversation, need to make it our focus to hear and understand the message before we respond.

We listen with not just our ears, but with our heart and mind. Active listening taking place with an open heart and an open mind makes it possible for the message to be received as the speaker intended without noise. The noise happens when the listener hears the message and then appends a judgment, feeling, emotion, belief, or opinion, which then distorts the meaning of the message.

Here is an example of when noise distorts a message. A person (the customer) is speaking to car salesperson 2 about an incident that took place when salesperson 1 insisted on showing a car they could not afford to buy. The customer still needs to buy a car and wants to be understood by a car salesperson who cares about them and wants to fulfill their need for being shown a car they can afford. Car salesperson 2 hears the story and starts thinking about how less of a commission they will make because the customer is on a budget. In response, they make a gesture that is off-putting to the customer and the customer walks away.

Now here is the same example when noise does not distort a message. Customer speaks to car salesperson 2 about the incident that took place with car salesperson 1. Car salesperson 2 seeks to understand with an open mind and heart, intently and intentionally listening to the customer. Car salesperson 2 responds with "I am so sorry you have yet to see the car that meets your budget, let me take you to these rows of cars you might like to see." Now, the customer feels heard, understood, and secure in knowing their needs will be met by car salesperson 2. Now that the customer is at ease, the purchase transaction is likely to take place, and maybe there's a chance of an upsell, with no pressure.

4.4 Ways to Engage Listeners

An interesting quote attributed to La Monte Young, an American performance artist, reads thus: *"If listeners aren't carried away to Heaven, I'm failing."* As a sales representative of your company or a team leader, if your listeners are not quite excited about what you are saying, you are only wasting your time. A sales representative should be able to create an entirely new sensation in the minds of customers/consumers listening to him or her. In the same way, for a company executive to convey sensitive and important data/information about the company to his/her employees, he/she must reach out to them in a way that will arouse their strong interest in what is being said.

Smooth communication takes place when people are fed with information they are mostly fascinated by. Therefore, there are technically four methods to give to people (customers, partners, investors, etc.) exactly what they will love to hear:

a. **Using the right tones:** People respond to different tones, and it is your sole responsibility as a business communicator to select the most appropriate tone to address someone if you want to get their attention. It is simply a commonsense thing; you can never talk to a baby boomer the way you will chat up a millennial. Your words will be regarded as rude and inappropriate to be reckoned with. It is also believed that when discussing with those who are highly educated, it is not advisable to use slang or lingos that they will consider very offensive.

b. **Meeting listeners' expectations:** If your speech or discussion holds no important meaning to your listeners, you are going to see them disappear from your presence in no time. Imagine what kind of response you will get when discussing investment in Bitcoin or cryptocurrencies with a senior citizen or discussing university courses with elementary school kids. The bottom line is that your messages should reflect the expectations of your listeners in order to keep them rooted to their seats and make them listen to you endlessly.

c. **Selecting the appropriate mode of delivery:** To succeed in oral communication, businesses need to respect people's choices when it comes to the way they want to be contacted. If one of your customers likes being visited personally from time to time, you should expect that such a customer may become unresponsive if you try to email or call him/her.

d. **Focusing on diction (choice of words):** Oral communication is primarily about selecting the right words to express an idea or transmit information from one person to another. The language employed in conversations or discussions can either impress or offend the listeners. If you experience being disrespected or your listeners run away while you are talking or delivering a speech, chances are that you may have used some annoying words or broken decorum by rudely addressing people. Abusive slang or slogans have no place in effective oral business communication. You are talking to human beings who are mostly emotional and could be offended at any time by whatever you may be saying.

4.5 7 Cs of Oral Communication

The good news is that business communicators can take some decisive actions to boost their oral communication. They can apply the following 7 Cs of effective oral communication to significantly improve their communication capability:[10]

a. **Clarity:** Before you can genuinely connect with your listeners/audience, your words and expressions must be very clear to them. Nothing is communicated when people struggle to understand or digest the information you are trying to pass across, no matter how important such information is. Therefore, try your best to make yourself very clear and use words/expressions your listeners are familiar with. Utilizing obscured expressions or technical terminologies that can put your listeners in the dark won't advance your communication in any way.

b. **Correctness:** Your message must be correct and factual. An organization that spreads false information is doing so at the risk of having its image or reputation battered by the public. Customers and business associates will avoid dealing with such an organization.

c. **Completeness:** As the saying goes, *"Half-truths are no truths"*. If you want to pass any information across to your internal and external stakeholders, it is imperative that the information be complete and understandable to the recipients.

---

10. Scheiber, H.J., and Hager, P.J. ((1994). Oral Communication in Business and Industry: Results of a Survey on Scientific, Technical, and Managerial Presentations. *Journal of Technical Writing and Communication*, 24(2), p171-173. https://doi.org/10.2190/W6LD-UPHF-K3BU-B23N

d. **Concreteness:** When a piece of information is concrete, it contains only facts and they are usually direct and solid. Telling old-fabled tales or releasing unconvincing information will only complicate a company's relationship with its stakeholders. This will increase misunderstandings that may tear them apart and abruptly end their business relationships. Therefore, an individual/organization may lose credibility if the information conveyed orally is not correct or appropriate.

e. **Conciseness:** The beauty of business communication is that it should be concise—this means that it should be short and straight to the point. There is no room to entertain the recipients while exchanging vital business information. Go straight to the point and convince your audience. The best approach anyone can use in achieving conciseness in communication is to always focus on what matters and ignore the noises or unnecessary information.

f. **Consideration:** Even though a company has all the right to send whatever messages it deems necessary to its employees, customers, investors, or partners, the messages must be considerate. This can be achieved by using tender and respectful language and tone in the messages.

g. **Courtesy:** No one listens to or pays attention to rude words employed in conveying a piece of information. Imagine an angry company's CEO speaking harshly to one of its customers or investors. We understand that such an attitude lacks due courtesy and may automatically end the relationship between the company and those who are offended by the tone of such CEO's communication.

Quiz

1. **How important is oral communication in the business community?**

   a. Less important

   b. Very important

   c. Not important at all

2. **Which of these is not a common type of oral communication?**

   a. Telephone conversation

   b. Social media browsing

   c. Face-to-face communication

3. **What does face-to-face communication indicate?**

   a. Sending an email to your friend

   b. Sitting down to talk one-on-one with a person

   c. Making a call

4. **How many types of listeners are discussed in this book?**

   a. 10

   b. 5

   c. 4

5. **Which kind of listeners are mostly searching for facts in every communication and may not necessarily be interested in being entertained?**

   a. Evaluative listeners

   b. Passive listeners

   c. Non-listeners

6. **What separates active listeners from passive listeners is that they listen almost to _____ of what is being said.**

   a. 15-20 percent

   b. 0 percent

   c. 90-100 percent

7. **Which of these attempts is one of the ways to meet listeners' expectations?**

   a. Telling them what will excite them

   b. Telling them lies

   c. Not telling them anything

8. **What does "diction" mean in oral communication?**

   a. Telephone

   b. Choice of words

   c. Playing music

9. **In what way does "diction" increase listeners' participation in oral communication?**

   a. If the communicator uses appropriate words, they will be interested in his/her messages.

   b. If the communicator knows how to dance, they will dance with him/her.

   c. People like listening to difficult vocabularies.

10. **Which of these messages uses the right, formal tone when talking with an investor?**

   a. Hello, Sir, how are you doing?

   b. Hey you, what's up?

   c. Hi, Buddy.

Answers	1 – b	2 – b	3 – b	4 – c	5 – a
	6 – c	7 – a	8 – b	9 – a	10 – a

Chapter Summary

◆ There are three major types of oral communication: Face-to-face communication, telephone conversations, and meeting discussions.

◆ Listeners to oral communication must be approached in a manner they will respond to, using the right tones, diction, mode of delivery, and meeting the listeners' expectations.

◆ There are 7 proven ways to boost oral communication, and they include the delivery of oral information that is clear, concise, concrete, correct, complete, courteous, and considerate.

◆ Oral communication is considered to be a very useful tool that enables communicators and their audience/ listeners to engage heart-to-heart with one another.

Chapter **5**

Types of Business Messages

Businesses/companies communicate different types of messages to their audience, whether they are internal or external. Each message contains important information that the company wants to send to its audience. In this chapter, efforts are made to distinctly describe the different types of business messages, their intrinsic characteristics, and why would a company want to release such a message to its audience.

Key learning objectives should include the reader's understanding of the following:

- Routine business messages
- Persuasive business messages
- Goodwill business messages
- Bad-news business messages

5.1 Routine Business Messages

As its name implies, routine business messages are a bulk of day-to-day information that a business may want to share with its internal and external stakeholders. It is up to the company to choose the format for delivering these routine messages because they could be delivered by emails, phone calls, or scheduled meetings.[11]

An organization exchanges routine messages with related stakeholders in the areas they are active towards the day-to-day operation of the organization. For example, a company's routine business messages to its internal stakeholders (employees, managers, team supervisors, executives, etc.) may contain information about:

a. Working guidelines or company's modus operandi

b. Project management instructions

c. Orsder executions and confirmations

d. Productivity surveys

e. Internal news and announcements

f. Human Resources (HR) updates, etc.

Similarly, some of the routine business messages an organization can transmit to its external stakeholders (investors, suppliers, customers, law enforcement, etc.) may include but are not limited to:

a. Contracts

b. Memorandum of Understanding (MOU) letters

---

11. Bovee, C.L., and Thill, J.V. (2020). *Business communication today.* London: Pearson, p.44.

c. Press releases

d. Financial data/information

e. Product/service catalog

f. Service letters

g. Product/service manuals, etc.

While writing a routine business message, it is advisable to pay attention to the following points:

- It must be addressed to a specific recipient.

- It is written to advance a certain aspect of the business's daily operations. For example, a project manager can send a memo to engineers about how to accomplish a task.

- It must be action-oriented and have a timeline for execution. In other words, the content of a routine business message must be carried out swiftly.

5.2 Persuasive Business Messages

Typically, persuasive business messages are those that are carefully designed to persuade some stakeholders associated with a business to take immediate action. Some common examples of persuasive business messages include

a. Sales/promotional messages

b. Persuasive customer claims

c. Request for proposals (RFPs) (for suppliers)

d. Request-for-action messages

e. Projects' Action Plans

f. Request-for-investment messages

To serve the purpose for which it was written, a persuasive business message must align with the expectations of the audience. That is, it must be positive and culturally appropriate. More so, the language used must be respectful and considerate. If the language is harsh and too urgent, it might give the audience the wrong impression that you or your business is desperate to get their money at all costs. A persuasive message should also adopt a tone that suits the work culture of the company and/or keep in mind any cultural differences that may be present between the company and the intended audience for the message. Most people won't respond to any call-to-action messages that don't add value to their lives and/or businesses. Even though the message is expected to be persuasive, its tone must still be gentle and courteous. Using your credibility smartly to persuade people can be a good strategy to write an effective persuasive message.

It is advisable that companies ask themselves these six strategic questions before writing/drafting their persuasive messages:

- What's the main idea/information the message is conveying to the audience?

- How will the message solve a current problem/pain point the targeted audience is experiencing?

- Why now?

- How does the audience want to be approached?

- What interesting story must be included in the message to excite the audience?

- What's the final response expected from the audience?

Depending on who (customers, investors, employees, etc.) a company wants to send a persuasive message to, the content can vary from one scenario to another. However, the most important thing is that the audience/recipients of such persuasive messages must have the positive impression that the sender (a company in this case) has some kind of consideration for them and the message is a credible way to propose solutions to certain problems they may be confronting.

5.3 Goodwill Business Messages

Sometimes a company may want to show appreciation to its employees, partners, investors, customers, etc. for their helpful contributions to the company's success by sending them some goodwill messages. As a matter of fact, an organization that has employees may periodically send some of the goodwill messages highlighted below, depending on the circumstances:[12]

- Thank-You notes

- Messages about in-company promotion (rank)

- Messages of appreciation

- Congratulatory messages

- Expressions of sympathy/condolence messages

In the same way, a company can send Thank-You notes or congratulatory messages to its customers, investors, partners, and so on. The primary purposes of goodwill messages are to motivate

---

12. Bovee, C.L., and Thill, J.V. (2018). *Business communication essentials: Fundamental skills for the mobile-digital-social workplace.* London: Pearson, p. 82.

stakeholders, demonstrate empathy, and strengthen existing relationships with the other parties. A goodwill message can be sent as a letter, email, or even delivered by a phone call.

A typical goodwill business message may look like this:

Sender address/date

Dear Victor,

In my official capacity as the Chief Executive Officer (CEO) of this company, I am glad to inform you about your promotion from Regional Sales Manager to National Sales Manager.

You would be entitled to all benefits and remuneration attached to your new position effective from today, 23 October, 2023.

Accept my sincere congratulations and I wish you all the best in your new position.

Dave Capella,
Chief Executive Officer (CEO),
Lotus Farms, Inc.

5.4 Bad-news (Negative) Business Messages

It is not every time that a company has good news to share with both its internal and external stakeholders. Sometimes the company's operations may be unexpectedly affected by uncontrollable natural disasters. Even inflation or poor national economic policies can hamper an organization's business activities. Unfortunately, not everything that happens to a company can be avoided or prevented by its management. For instance, when there is a tornado at the place where a company's manufacturing plant is located, some equipment or machinery belonging to the company may be destroyed in the process.

In spite of the fact that bad-news business messages are disheartening, it is advisable that the messages are cautiously worded so that they won't produce negative reactions from employees and other parties connected to the company.

Therefore, the best approach for delivering bad-news messages to an organization's stakeholders requires that the messages must be concise, factual, and direct, and they need to state clearly what efforts the organization's management is taking to rebuild the business systems to lessen the effects of the bad news on its business operations.

Below are some checklists to consider while writing bad news or negative business messages[13]:

- **Explain clearly and completely -** Your message should not be confusing for the readers. Write with clarity so that readers can understand and accept the bad news.

- **Use a professional tone -** It is important to adopt a calm, polite, and professional tone. Readers of bad news messages will often be enraged or disturbed and you should know how to handle this situation.

---

13. Pavy, Jeanne, and Veronika Humphries. "Chapter 6: Routine Messages." Strategies for Effective Business Communication, August 1, 2022. https://louis.pressbooks.pub

- **Be sensitive and empathetic** - Respect and empathy can greatly help reduce bad feelings among recipients. Accept blame and apologize wherever appropriate.

- **Be fair** - Your bad news message must reinforce that the decision taken was fair, rational, and in everyone's best interests.

- **Maintain friendly relations** - You must demonstrate your desire to continue pleasant relations with the receivers and to regain their confidence.

Quiz

1. **There are basically _____ types of business messages.**

    a. 5

    b. 4

    c. 8

2. **Which of these is not a typical example of a routine business message?**

    a. Congratulatory message

    b. Project management instructions

    c. Productivity surveys

3. **A condolence message is an example of _____**

    a. Routine business message

    b. Persuasive business message

    c. Goodwill business message

4. **When a company requests that its investors should provide more funds to finance its business activities. This is an example of _____**

    a. Persuasive business message

    b. Goodwill message

    c. Routine message

5. **When there is a natural disaster that affects the activities of an organization, its management can send a _____ to all its workers and partners.**

   a. Bad-news message

   b. Goodwill message

   c. Persuasive message

6. **All of these except one is a routine message that a company can send to its external stakeholders.**

   a. Contracts

   b. Memorandum of Understanding (MOU)

   c. Condolence letter

7. **Employees as well as customers like Thank-You Notes. Thank-You Notes are _____**

   a. Bad-news messages

   b. Persuasive messages

   c. Goodwill messages

8. **Mr. James Kent recently got promoted into a new position in his company. What kind of business message is he likely to receive from his employer?**

   a. Bad-news message

   b. Goodwill message

   c. Persuasive message

9. If you are a project manager, you would like to give some instructions to your subordinates so that they know exactly what to do with the project. You are surely going to send them a _____

    a. Goodwill message

    b. Routine message

    c. Bad-news message

10. "Congratulations on your new car!" One company's senior executive said to one of his/her junior staff. That was a _____

    a. Bad-news message

    b. Goodwill message

    c. Persuasive message

Answers	1 – b	2 – a	3 – c	4 – a	5 – a
	6 – c	7 – c	8 – b	9 – b	10 – b

Chapter Summary

◆ There are four major types of business messages: Routine, persuasive, goodwill, and bad-news (negative) messages.

◆ Routine messages are the regular or usual messages organizations send to their employees, partners, or customers about their business's operations.

◆ Persuasive messages are fundamentally used to request for a particular favor, whether from an employee or an investor.

◆ Goodwill messages are used to express good feelings and kind considerations between organizations and their stakeholders.

◆ When something bad unexpectedly happens to a company, the news could be contained in a bad news message sent to its stakeholders.

Chapter 6

Everyday Business Communication Tools

Today, organizations have access to several communication tools that they can utilize in connecting with their employees, customers, partners, etc. Memos, emails, letters, and business plans are the four primary tools used in business communication, in addition to telephones. This chapter provides detailed descriptions and the usefulness of these four main business communication tools.

The key learning objectives of this chapter should include the reader's understanding of the following:

- What are memos and how are they used in the digital world

- The use of emails and the difference between a good and bad email

- The do's and don'ts of business letters

- Business plans and their usefulness in startup culture

6.1 Memos

A memo is the shortened form of the word "Memorandum". A business memo is a written document used by businesses or organizations to communicate a piece of information to people within and outside the business/company. In this case, a memo can be used in passing some actionable instructions across to employees, investors, suppliers, and so on. There are different types of business memorandums (memos), and some of them are highlighted as follows:

- **Request memo:** This memo is sent out to request a favor or some assistance. A team leader can send a request memo to one of the employees they supervise for some help. In the same way, a company's CEO can send a memo to one of his company's investors for additional funds or support. For a request memo to be effective, it must clearly state the intended request, and what exact actions the writer of the memo expects. It is important to always remember that the language used in a request memo must be formal and courteous. A courteous tone is favorable to everyone and does not show arrogance.

- **Confirmation memo:** A company's CEO/President may write a confirmation memo to confirm something that has been previously agreed upon in words or prior memos.

When writing a confirmation memo, it is imperative to specifically mention previous agreements on the issue, and the modalities for achieving the agreements must be highlighted. If necessary, you should request for your partner's or recipient's feedback and/or contributions to the process. If you have some gray areas about the agreements that you need further clarification on, ask for the recipients' inputs through the memo.

- **Suggestive memo:** Senior executives in an organization may want to ask their subordinates about how to solve a particular problem the organization is facing. A suggestive memo is the best tool for this. Workers in the same departments can seek contributions from one another to find some practical solutions that their departments currently require.

Technically, a memo is a communication tool for mass information. It can be sent from a senior executive to junior employees/staffers in a company (this is considered a "downward memo"). A memo can likewise be sent from the junior workers to a senior manager or executive within the same company (this is called an "upward memo"). However, when a couple of employees who have the same rank or hold the same position in a company send a memo to each other, this is usually referred to as a "horizontal memo".

Figure 6.1 shows a sample memo template. You can download a ready-to-use version of this template from the Online Resources available with this book.

Figure 6.1   **A memo template**

	LOGO
	LETTERHEAD OF THE COMPANY

Memorandum

To: _____

From: _____

Date: _____

Subject: _____

(Paragraph 1: Inform what the memo is about. Keep it short and to the point.)

(Paragraph 2: Provide any additional information or context.)

(Paragraph 3: Close the memo with a call to action.)

6.1.1 Sending memos in a digitalized world

Memos are still regarded as an effective communication tool in many organizations. However, in our digitalized workplaces, several digital alternatives are being utilized instead of memos in some organizations. These include the company's intranet, group/business instant messaging applications/software/ and, of course, the company's email.[14]

A paper memo still holds the prestige of being seen as a branded piece of document, bearing the well-designed name, logo, and contact information of the organization sending it. On the other hand, digital instant messaging applications can do exactly what paper memos are used for—sending timely and applicable information within an organization, or from the organization to some recipients located outside but are connected to the sender in one way or the other.

Some examples of useful instant messaging applications/software employed for both internal and external memo-like business communication are:

- **Slack:** As a collaborative application, an organization can use Slack to speedily notify, update, and pass important instructions from one of its departments to the others in real-time. That is what a memo could be used for. The applicable external recipients must be onboarded within the organization's Slack ecosystem to be able to receive direct and swift notifications or updates from the organizations. It also has additional features such as calling and file sharing.

- **Skype:** Primarily designed as a calling client/software, Skype now has almost the same functionalities as Slack

---

14. Dwyer, J., and Hopwood, N. (2019). *The business communication handbook.* Victoria: Cengage Learning Australia, p. 16.

and other collaborative software. An organization can send instant messages and share files with its stakeholders using Skype.

- **Google Workspace:** This is a central workspace designed by Google for businesses/organizations, making it possible for them to combine their emails, calling (video or audio), word processing (doc), file sharing (drive), and organization (calendar, etc.) on one single dashboard. Organizations could also utilize all paid and unpaid Android applications.

- **Microsoft Teams:** Microsoft Teams works exactly like Google Workspace, with some additional useful applications developed by Microsoft.

Digital memos can be sent more quickly than paper memos, and the response time could be shortened as well; in other words, recipients of memos can choose to reply to them immediately, unlike replies to paper memos that may take some time and are required to be posted.

6.2 Emails

Just like a memo, the greatest benefit businesses gain from using emails as a business communication tool is that it offers them the rare chance to connect with more than one recipient at a time. Emails can be crafted like every other business message, but they should include a short but self-explanatory subject line. An email also makes it possible to share a file/document that contains additional information as an attachment. Communication experts believe that powerful business communication emails should be:

- Simple to read and digest by the recipients

- Logical and specifically address the issue it is written about

- Short and direct—long emails bore recipients like an uninteresting movie!

- Respectful—never send an abusive email to anyone, even when you have been previously offended by any of the recipients

- Reasonable and empathetic/sympathetic

Your emails will be received by another human being like you. So, it is just a matter of common sense to be empathetic to the cause the email is written about and show some consideration to the recipient (s).

6.2.1 Differences between good and bad emails

With all the benefits of emails, which include but are not limited to faster reach across various geographical locations and easy storage and retrieval procedures, an organization may still end up sending bad emails to either its internal or external stakeholders.

Efforts are provided below to explain what could make an email good or bad:

- **Partial content:** A good email has all the necessary information that the recipient(s) needs to make an informed decision about something. On the other hand, a bad email contains scanty information and may leave the recipient confused and desirous of additional information.

- **Sloppy structure:** When an email has a poor or ineffective opening line, too many capitalizations, unrelated images, and other media, and lacks an appropriate subject/title, or is written in a rude, unrespectful tone, it can be considered to be bad. A good email is just the opposite of that!

- **Full of mistakes:** A bad email will be full of grammatical and spelling errors to the point that the recipients may misunderstand parts or all the information in the message. On the contrary, a good email is clean, well-written, and clearly expresses the purpose (s) for which it is written.

6.3 Letters

Writing business letters has been the norm or the normal practice for years, but there are some helpful tips that can be incorporated into your letter writing to ensure it does exactly what you want it to do. Whether you are writing a cover letter, congratulatory letter, complaint letter, memo, or acknowledgment letter, you can make your business letters stand out by taking the following strategic steps:

- Use a distinctive letterhead that precisely depicts your business's style and brand

- Utilize the appropriate language and tone—Formal language for formal letters, informal language for informal letters

- Never forget to indicate the date the letter is written on

- Make use of the right salutations (greetings) based on the types of recipients you are targeting. Formal letters should start with "Dear Sir/Madam" and end with "Yours faithfully/Yours sincerely". On the contrary, informal letters can start with just "Hi/Hello" and be ended with "Yours/It's me/It's your pal, etc.")

- Go straight to the point after the initial greetings and elaborate on them in the letter's body

- Finally, don't forget to append signatures to your formal letters. Signature also adds authority to your letters

6.4 Business Plans

Very few business owners fully understand how important their business plans are. We are now in the startup culture/movement, and business plans are playing a very important and strategic role in communication, most especially between business owners and potential investors or suppliers. In addition to using it as a guideline for how they want to run their business's daily operations, business plans are also a form of business communication tool.[15] There are different types of business plans: The mini plan, presentation plan (a pitch deck), the working (operational) plan, and what-if (contingency) plan. Each of these business plans communicates certain information/messages to investors and partners about a business.

When you show your business plan to investors, you are inadvertently revealing vital information about your business to them. They can easily learn about how you intend to run your business activities and eventually profit from those actions.

---

15. Perkins, P.S. (2010). *The art and science of communication tools for effective communication in the workplace.* London: Wiley, p. 47.

6.4.1 The usefulness of a business plan in the startup culture

Since 2012, according to Crunchbase news (shown in Figure 6.2 below), the amount venture capitalists have invested in North American startups or small businesses increased from less than $100 billion in 2012 to over $300 billion in 2021.

Figure 6.2　**North American Venture Dollar Volume 2012-2021**

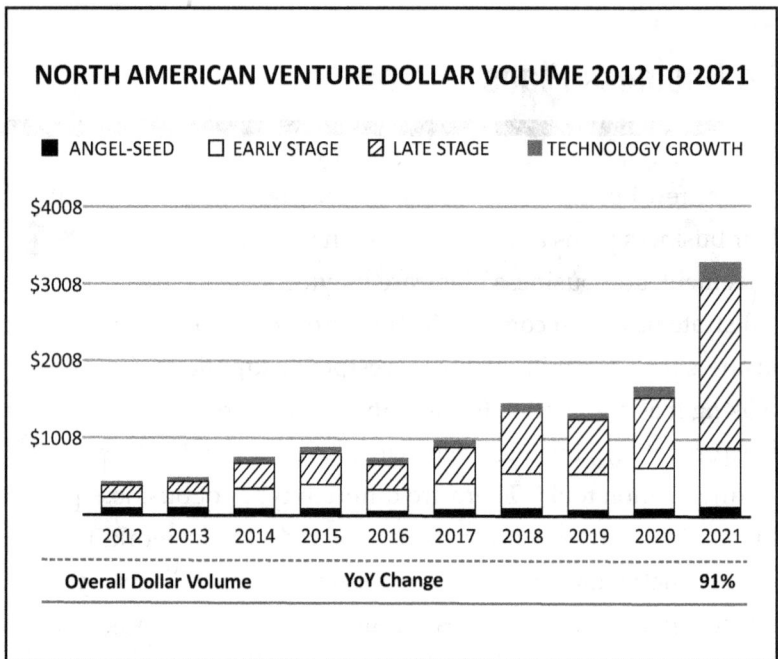

NORTH AMERICAN VENTURE DOLLAR VOLUME 2012 TO 2021

■ ANGEL-SEED　☐ EARLY STAGE　▨ LATE STAGE　▪ TECHNOLOGY GROWTH

2012	2013	2014	2015	2016	2017	2018	2019	2020	2021

$4008 — $3008 — $2008 — $1008

Overall Dollar Volume	YoY Change	91%

Source: news.crunchbase.com[16]

Within the startup ecosystem, the very first document for business communication between businesses and their prospective investors is a pitch deck or a presentation business plan. It is

---

16. Glasner, Joanna. "North American Startup Funding Scaled Unprecedented Heights in 2021." Crunchbase News, January 21, 2022. https://news.crunchbase.com

almost impossible for a startup to convince any venture capitalist to part with their hard-earned money without a well-prepared, factual, and applicable presentation business plan. A well-designed pitch deck must contain the following essential elements:

- A brief introduction

- A problem statement

- A solution statement

- A market analysis

- A business model

- A marketing plan

- Financial projections

- Traction and revenue

The startup culture has come to stay, spreading from one corner of the world to the other, and it will be required of every small business/startup that desires to raise venture capital or get investors' money to communicate its missions/goals to the potential investor via its presentation business plan.

Quiz

1. **Why is a business plan the least used communication tool in the business community until now?**

   a. Some business owners don't like having business plans

   b. Because most business owners don't understand that their business plans are communication tools

   c. Because most businesses don't need business plans

2. **Apart from telephones, there are _____ main communication tools businesses often use in their day-to-day operations.**

   a. 5

   b. 8

   c. 4

3. **Memo is actually a shortened form of the word _____**

   a. Manmade

   b. Memorandum

   c. Memory

4. **Which of these is not an example of memos?**

   a. Social media

   b. Suggestive memo

   c. Confirmation memo

5. As the President of your company, if you want your employees to do something for you, you will need to send a _____ to them.

   a. Suggestive memo

   b. Request memo

   c. Confirmation memo

6. What is another name for a presentation business plan?

   a. Financial statement

   b. Pitch deck

   c. Marketing plan

7. Why do startups need a pitch deck nowadays?

   a. For hiring their employees

   b. For selling their products/services

   c. For raising money from venture capitalists/investors

8. What is great about emails as a communication tool?

   a. It cannot be sent to many recipients at the same time

   b. It can contain additional information as attachments

   c. It is very slow

9. **A good email MUST NOT have** _____

   a. Full content

   b. Many mistakes

   c. A subject/title

10. **When using letters as a communication tool, you should have a** _____

   a. An email address

   b. A letterhead

   c. A computer

Answers	1 – b	2 – c	3 – b	4 – a	5 – b
	6 – b	7 – c	8 – b	9 – b	10 – b

Chapter Summary

◆ Apart from telephones, there are four main traditional communication tools adopted by almost every organization. They are memos, emails, letters, and business plans.

◆ Memo, a shortened form of the word "memorandum" is a mass information tool that a company can send to all its employees and external stakeholders at once.

◆ In the same way, emails can pass information from one end of an organization to the other, and they can include files and other documents as attachments.

◆ Letters have always been around, and businesses continue to use this medium to exchange very important information with their stakeholders.

◆ Business plans are the least used communication tool because many business owners do not necessarily recognize their business plans as viable business communication tools. However, nowadays, startups that want to raise some venture capital must present their convincing presentation business plans to their potential investors.

This page is intentionally left blank

Chapter **7**

Business Proposals, Reports, and Presentations

Organizations put their powerful messages or information to be delivered to their employees, customers, investors, partners, or even law enforcement in proposals, reports, and/or presentations. Sometimes, how information is presented to others is as important as the information itself. Imagine how an investor, a business partner, or even a customer will respond to a shoddily prepared and poorly designed report, with many spelling or typographic mistakes! On most occasions, they will put the poorly presented report or proposal away, since they don't feel excited about reading an unclear and confusing report. Then what happens? The company that prepared that poor-quality report had lost a rare opportunity to connect or communicate with one of its principal stakeholders.

The key learning objectives of this chapter should include the reader's understanding of the following:

- Researching and planning your proposals, reports, and presentations

- Drafting and completing your proposals, reports, and presentations

- Delivering your proposals, reports, and presentations

7.1 Researching and Planning Your Proposals, Reports, and Presentations

Proposals are business documents an organization sends to another business or organization to persuade it to enter into a form of business relationship with it, whether to buy its products/services or supply its much-needed raw materials. A business report documents the business activities an organization undertakes to inform its employees, partners, investors, etc. about the progress the organization is making. A business presentation gives an organization the unique opportunity to clearly explain certain aspects of its operations to its employees, customers, partners, investors, etc.

In order to produce a high-quality proposal, report, or presentation that communicates clearly and efficiently, the writer must carry out some necessary research and plan how to incorporate the research findings in the context of the proposal, report, or presentation.

Highlighted below are five techniques for researching for a business report, proposal, or presentation:

- **Subject matter:** What kind of message do you want to pass across to the report or proposal readers? Is it about a new product/service recently developed by your company? How will such a product/service be useful to the readers? At the same time, you may want to update your customers, for example, about certain information they had previously received from you. What was the previous information/ message? What has changed since the first information/ message was delivered to them? Whether you are writing a business report or presentation, the first thing to consider is finding out the "what" that will be presented in it. The "what" is that special information or subject-matter you think your readers will receive excitedly. Without first discovering the "what", your report will become floppy, consisting of no concrete message that your readers can gladly use in improving the existing relationship between you and them. And the subject matter should be about the solutions you are delivering to your readers/listeners.

- **Tone and language:** You may need to spend some time selecting the most appropriate tone or language to be used in your reports or proposals. This step is quite necessary if you are dealing with an entirely new kind of audience. For example, you are invited as a business manager of a company to deliver a presentation to a group of potential investors. Your primary responsibility is to ensure that your amazing audience is treated nicely and respectfully (not rudely with expletive-filled rants). This is why it becomes imperative to research the appropriate words and tone to use in arousing their collective interest in whatever you are going to tell them.

- **Call-to-action:** While researching for a report or presentation meant for customers or investors, you may need to focus on using proper calls-to-action. It is technically wrong to send a report to an investor with a call-to-action that he/she should "try out our products!". Similarly, your customers will be alarmed to receive a report from you that contains the call-to-action, "We would appreciate your investment in our company!". As much as every report, proposal, or presentation has at least one call-to-action, it is crucial to research the most appropriate one in order not to confuse the mind of the person reading the report.

- **Method/Format of delivery:** Before writing your report or presentation, you will save yourself a lot of time by knowing first how you are going to deliver it or how the recipient would love to be contacted. Each delivery method requires different approaches. Hence, to do it properly, spend some time to ascertain the delivery method. Will it be by email, letter, online presentation, etc. Once you've discovered how your audience prefers to be contacted, you can then customize your report or presentation accordingly.

- **Connecting the dots:** At this point in time, you would like to connect all the dots, so to say, about everything the audience has known about your company and its products/ services. Have you sent some reports to them in the past? How did the content in those reports relate to or align with the current one you are preparing to write? If the report or proposal recipient is an entirely new business associate, how much do they already know about you and your company? Effectively, joining the dots (bringing all necessary information into one piece of message) helps you to come up with robust, detailed business communication that could open the doors for more business interactions as well as create new businesses for you and them.

7.2 Drafting and Completing Your Proposals, Reports, and Presentations

In this section, efforts are deployed toward explaining all the necessary steps you should take so as to produce very effective business proposals, reports, and presentations.

7.2.1 Writing a business proposal

Starting with a business proposal, it is an undeniable fact that there is no one-size-fits-all approach to drafting powerful business proposals.[17] However, there is a pattern that is common to all business proposals, and they are outlined below:

- **Define your problem:** You need to define the problem or pain point that the business proposal aims to solve. You should consider this as your hook that will instantly draw the proposal readers into the proposal. When people see the same issue they are dealing with mentioned in a proposal, they will be excited about reading the remaining parts of the proposal.

- **Present your solution (s):** Go ahead and offer your solutions to the readers' problems or concerns. We all love hearing good news, most especially the ones that will help us eliminate our pain points.

17. Forsyth, P. (2016). *How to write reports and proposals*. London: Kogan Page, p.77.

- **Distinguish your deliverables and highlight success rates:** It is not enough to tell proposal readers that you've got the best solutions to their problems, also you must take a step further to distinguish your deliverables from the others already in the market. You can talk excitedly about your success rates—that is, confidently explain how useful and effective your solutions are.

- **Describe your approaches:** It is also necessary to clearly state your approach or procedures for utilizing your solutions to benefit your readers.

- **Seek readers' cooperation/participation:** If applicable, remind your readers of their previous expressions of interest in your products/services. Press them to take the required actions in exploring the benefits offered by your products/services for their own good.

- **Hopeful conclusion:** Conclude your proposal on a hopeful note by asking or imploring your readers to make decisions to purchase your products or use your services or imploring your readers to make business decisions as quickly as possible.

- **Edit/proofread your proposal:** It is not sensible to send a poorly written business proposal to people. It may discourage them from reading it or believing what was written in it. Spend time to proofread and edit your proposal. If necessary, you can hire an external proofreader/ editor to have a second look at your proposal if your company doesn't have in-house content editors.

7.2.2 Some common mistakes while writing a business proposal

- **It is not client-focused** - The proposal should be drafted keeping in mind the audience it is to be presented to. Keeping it client-focussed will ensure the client's interest is managed.

- **It is similar to competitors** - While it is important to research competitors, your business proposal should be unique and hold a different value from your competitors.

- **It is not credible** - Ensure that your business proposal establishes the credibility of your organization.

- **It promises an inaccurate budget** - It is not a good idea to present an inaccurate budget knowing that it may change. Conduct in-depth research and provide a budget that is as accurate as possible.

- **It doesn't give a clear plan or solution** - Your business proposal should provide a clear solution to the pain points and a clear plan about how you aim to achieve it.

- **The solution does not match the purpose** - Ensure that your solution solves the pain points that were described at the start and does not deviate from the topic.

7.2.3 Writing a business report

If you aim to write a formal and powerful business report, these eleven action steps will be quite helpful to you:[18]

---

18. Taylor, N. (2014). *Business express: Writing compelling reports and proposals: Creating content that informs, engages, and persuades.* Harlow, UK: Pearson Education Limited.

1. **Spend some time on planning:** This may involve choosing all the context you want to see in the report as well as deciding on other important elements of an effective business report described below.

2. **Select the appropriate format for your report:** If your company has a standard format or template it has been using for some time and is not willing to replace it with a new template any time soon, use the existing template as it is. Consistency is a form of business branding.

3. **Add a befitting title:** The title should contain some keywords that are directly related to the main message. For example, if you use "three main products" as the title of your business report, this may confuse many of your readers. However, if you personalize or customize the title, it will send a stronger meaning to your report readers. For instance, "our company's three main products" is more sensible as a title than the previous one.

4. **Provide a table of contents:** You should have a useful and clear table of contents so that your readers can quickly glance through the context of the report. In this busy world, people don't have the time to read an entire report before finding out what it is all about.

5. **Add a summary or abstract:** Add a summary or an abstract to your report to give readers a peek into what they are going to discover in your report. It is generally believed that if the abstract is properly done, it will encourage readers to excitedly delve into the remaining parts of the report. On the contrary, a dull and uninviting abstract will cause readers not to show enough interest in reading the whole

report. So, pay attention to this fact so as not to produce an abstract that compels readers to throw away your business reports.

6. **Include an introduction:** Your report's introduction should immediately draw readers in. It should inform them about what to expect in the report. It should be short, sweet, and appealing. Writing a powerful introduction to your report is similar to welcoming a visitor to your office with warm, open arms. In this case, first impressions matter a lot.

7. **Provide strategic steps to be taken:** Every business report, it turns out, is about releasing new or updated information or offering the much-needed solution to a problem. If your report details the benefits of your product/service, it is helpful to your readers to provide some strategic steps or actions they should take to take advantage of the product/ service.

8. **Add testimonial stories and endorsements:** In the case of releasing a new product/service, it is appropriate to include testimonial stories or endorsements from other people who have already enjoyed using your product/service.

9. **Give conclusions and recommendations:** End your report in an upbeat mood. Make sure that your conclusion connects the dots of all the important points raised in the report. In certain cases, it may be essential to make some recommendations for your readers.

10. **Include bibliography and appendices:** Formal business reports that contain information or ideas obtained from secondary or external sources should have a bibliography. It depends on which reference style you are using. This can be referred to as "References" or "Works Cited". Your

appendices should have other supporting information that had gone into writing the main report but could not be included in the main section of the report due to lack of space. For example, a company may put its financial statement in a report's appendices, instead of including it inside the primary context of the report.

11. **Proofread, edit, and rewrite:** A beautifully written report doesn't just happen suddenly without making some conscious efforts; a powerful business report comes from proofreading, editing, and fine-tuning the first draft. As the saying goes, all great writings emanate from countless rewritings.

7.2.4 Writing a business presentation

There are five major types of business presentations: Sales pitch, keynote speech investor pitch, lecture, and new product/service release.

A sales pitch is the presentation a business gives to encourage others to purchase its products/services. Keynote speeches and lectures are periodically arranged by companies to promote certain values and/or socially beneficial programs. When eyeing to get some investors' money, an organization needs a very good investor pitch. Organizations inform their customers about their latest products or services by announcing their release through a newsletter or a press release.

All these kinds of business presentations have something in common; they comprise of five main parts:

1. **Introduction:** You are required to offer the preamble to the message or information you want to deliver in

your presentation. It is like providing a snapshot of the whole presentation to your audience. It is possible to use questions, anecdotes (short narratives), or quotes to introduce a subject-matter or an issue.

2. **Objective:** You may want to highlight the objective of your proposed presentation in a bullet format or you can list and number them. Your audience will surely be glad to know beforehand what salient points/issues you will deliver in your presentation. Think of it as your presentation's Table of Contents (TOCs).

3. **Overview:** Your presentation's overview is actually the summary of its main points/content. For example, if you are delivering a presentation about equal pay for both male and female employees, you may want to first provide a chart or a statistical illustration that currently shows that men are getting paid more than their female counterparts in different organizations. Then you can present a summary of how you intend to address this issue in your organization. In essence, you are giving your presentation a foreword.

4. **The main presentation:** This is where the major work is—you need to present concrete facts and data that will convincingly educate, inform, and encourage your audience. For simplicity's purpose, it is sensible to divide your presentation into chunks (small paragraphs) so that your audience can grab the main idea in each of them. Also, pay attention to your grammar and punctuation. Communication experts believe that short, concrete, and memorable sentences should replace long and windy sentences that may bore an audience. Nowadays, it is helpful to include appropriate graphics, pictures, and/or

illustrations in business presentations. People keep visual images in their memories longer than typed words.

5. **Summary/conclusion/references:** You will need a separate section for references if you have quoted statements or utilized ideas from other secondary sources. This will protect you from being accused of plagiarism which could affect your organization's reputation. More so, try to summarize the main contents of your presentation in the concluding section. Let your conclusion be concise, direct, and tight.

7.3 Delivering Your Proposals, Reports, and Presentations

There are three intrinsic methods for delivering business proposals, reports, or presentations.

1. **Oral delivery:** This means that you can directly deliver the content of your proposals or reports by talking about them with your listeners or audience. This can happen in meetings, conferences, seminars, etc. Figure 7.2 points out some common mistakes individuals can make while delivering their presentation orally.

Figure 7.2.   **4 Common mistakes when making a business presentation**

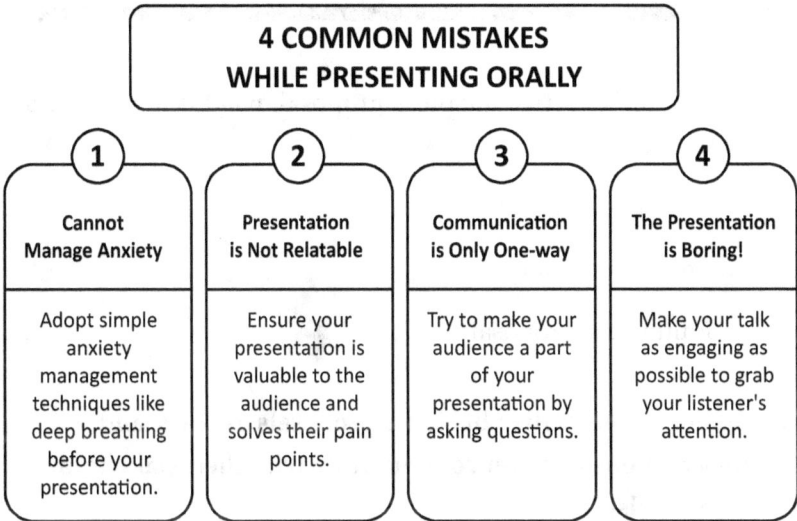

**4 COMMON MISTAKES
WHILE PRESENTING ORALLY**

1	2	3	4
Cannot Manage Anxiety	**Presentation is Not Relatable**	**Communication is Only One-way**	**The Presentation is Boring!**
Adopt simple anxiety management techniques like deep breathing before your presentation.	Ensure your presentation is valuable to the audience and solves their pain points.	Try to make your audience a part of your presentation by asking questions.	Make your talk as engaging as possible to grab your listener's attention.

Adapted from: eveash.com

2. **Written delivery:** Your written business proposals or reports can be emailed or physically distributed to your audience. This entails that your audience will have access to every detail of the report and digest them accordingly using their own discretions. That is, you won't be talking them into believing in the reports or presentations.

3. **Electronic delivery:** You can also deliver your business reports or proposals electronically by email, newsletters, blogs, website content, etc. Electronic delivery is fast and affordable.

Quiz

1. **To write an effective business proposal, what is the very first thing to do?**

   a. Problem definition

   b. Proposal delivery

   c. Editing the proposal

2. **Organizations utilize business proposals, reports, and presentations to better communicate with their stakeholders. True or false?**

   a. False

   b. True

3. **The most common method to deliver a report electronically is?**

   a. A letter

   b. An email

   c. A telephone call

4. **Which of these is NOT a method for delivering a business report or proposal nowadays?**

   a. Oral delivery

   b. Electronic delivery

   c. Robot delivery

5. **The main content of your business proposals, reports, and presentations is referred to as the _____**

   a. Tone and language

   b. Subject-matter

   c. Conclusion

6. **Which of these is considered to be an appropriate tone in a business proposal or report?**

   a. Courteous and respectful tone

   b. Rude tone

   c. Arrogant or proud tone

7. **What may happen if an investor receives a proposal that is shoddily prepared and full of grammatical errors?**

   a. The investor will enjoy reading it.

   b. The investor may not complete reading the proposal.

   c. The investor may not open it.

8. **The last part of a business report or presentation is usually called the "conclusion/recommendations". True or false?**

   a. False

   b. True

9. **Why does a report or presentation need a bibliography or reference section?**

   a. Because the content is not long enough

   b. Because it is important to give credit to the sources of the materials in it

   c. Because it is the first part of a report or presentation

10. **A "Table of Contents" (TOC) usually provides a list of topics and subtopics that are NOT written in a report or presentation. True or false?**

    a. True

    b. False

Answers	1 – a	2 – b	3 – b	4 – c	5 – b
	6 – a	7 – b	8 – b	9 – b	10 – b

Chapter Summary

◆ To create an effective business proposal, report, or presentation, the very first thing to do is to sit down and plan what to put in it.

◆ Without adequately planning what should be included in your proposals, reports, or presentations may result in producing sloppy content that has no significant benefit to offer to your audience or recipients.

◆ After that, you should carefully draft your proposal, report, or presentation. Most of the facts and details you will write in the document have already been obtained through the initial planning.

◆ Once you have completed a draft of your proposal, report, or presentation, you need to ruthlessly edit and proofread it to make sure it is error-free.

◆ The last step is to deliver your proposal, report, or presentation to the appropriate recipient. You can choose to do this electronically or physically.

This page is intentionally left blank

Chapter **8**

Employment Communication as a Form of Business Communication

Employment communication is now considered an integral aspect of business communication because it is basically conducted within a business setting or ecosystem. For example, a startup needs some employees to work for it. To achieve this, the startup management must engage in employing suitably qualified professionals for the positions open in their company. And there would definitely be back-and-forth communication between the startup and the job candidates who have already applied to work in the company. This explains why employment communication must be treated comprehensively in the business context because no company can operate by itself— it needs employees. On the other side, it is also important for prospective employees to learn effective communication strategies to build a strong first impression. This involves creating a crisp resume and cover letter and handling the interview process efficiently.

The key learning objectives of this chapter should include the reader's understanding of the following:

- How to best communicate your professional brand to your future employer

- Resume/Curriculum Vitae (CV) writing

- 10 important steps for crafting a successful job application cover letter

- Handling your pre-interview communication like a Pro

- Expectations from employers during employment communication

8.1 How To Best Communicate Your Professional Brand To Your Future Employer

As a job candidate seeking employment from a company, you stand a great chance of getting your dream job if you know how best to communicate your professional brand to your future employer. A person's professional brand comprises his/her academic qualifications, attitude, and skills. It is possible for someone to be highly educated and demonstrate enviable qualities; however, if they don't know how to present their professional brand to potential employers, their dream jobs may remain elusive.

When communicating your professional brand to a company that may hire you, pay attention to the following cogent points:

- **Showcasing your greatest skills and abilities:** Education is very important, and it will at least get your foot in the door. If a company is advertising to fill a position that requires a university/college degree, you'll meet that important requirement if you have already graduated from the college/university. In addition to that, you still need to demonstrate that you have the right skill set and admirable abilities. If an organization aspires to hire a frontend software developer, getting a degree in Computer Science will only get you in the door, but you still need to show that you have the required software development skills needed to function as a frontend software developer. Nowadays, some CEOs, including Elon Musk, Tesla's CEO, are looking to employ people with exceptional and creative abilities even though they didn't go to college. You may possess the appropriate certificate and skills, but it is still necessary to highlight only those essential skills you would need to carry out your duties at your targeted company/organization.

- **Evidence of past work:** Experience comes from doing something over a certain period. Almost all employers like to have experienced employees on their teams. Therefore, it is in your power to impress your potential employer by making references to some completed past work in the same field/industry. As a computer programmer, show your future employer some useful codes or projects you've successfully worked on. If you are an experienced salesperson or marketer, quote relevant statistics of how you've crushed your sales number in some other companies. Showing concrete evidence of well-executed past assignments is enough to convince your future employer that you know what you are doing and would deliver similar successes or even better if hired.

- **Great attitude and quality-mindedness:** The job market is now very competitive and employers are looking past academic qualifications and experiences to select workers who will culturally fit within their organizations. For the fact that every company has its own culture, the management of every company puts a premium on selecting job candidates that will advance their corporate cultures, not those who will come in to cause chaos. Hence, job applicants' attitudes or characters are one of the main criteria used by employers for choosing them or not. In addition to that, employers are also focusing on how quality-conscious their prospective employees will be. Before hiring, they set aside enough time to scrutinize job applicants' previous projects and work to ascertain that they could do quality work. As a job applicant, always present your best experiences or projects for potential employers to review. Highlight, in your resume/CV, your professional achievements while on your past jobs. Allow your future employers to see who they will be working with by highlighting clear and understandable past employment accomplishments.

- **Tell a good narrative/story:** Recruiters are encouraging job seekers to be good storytellers to get their next dream jobs. A storyteller? That's right! As a job candidate, you should be able to use the facts, experiences, and good commendations received in previous jobs or positions to tell a wonderful story or narrative that will convince your future recruiter/employer. Instead of just providing a bullet point of achievements in your past jobs in cover letters, you can weave them into a powerful story that can resonate with your targeted recruiter/employer. If you are dreaming of getting a job with Apple, Inc., for example, your story of how you creatively used your iPad or iPhone in your previous jobs could catch the recruiter's short-spanned attention.

8.2 Resume/Curriculum Vitae (CV)

You would need a resume/CV if you are applying for any job. This is a document that contains some brief information about your education, qualifications, experiences, a list of previous employers, and other important details you want your prospective employer to know.[19] It is usually sent alongside your job application or a cover letter.

There are different kinds of resumes/CVs, some common ones are described below:

- **Chronological resume:** This kind of resume focuses on the details of your previous job experiences or your work history. It could be longer than any other type of resume because you are required to provide the necessary information about all the past jobs you have ever had.

Figure 8.1 shows a sample chronological resume template. You can also download a ready-to-use resume template from the Online Resources available with this book.

---

19. McGee, P. (2014). *How to write a CV that really works: A concise, clear, and comprehensive guide to writing an effective CV.* London: Little Brown Book Group, p. 25.

- **Functional resume:** This type of resume mostly focuses on the skills and abilities that you have to successfully do the job you are applying for.

- **Combination resume:** In structure, this kind of resume looks like a combination of both functional and chronological resumes. It may run up to 5-7 pages in length or more, depending on your past job experiences and qualifications.

- **Infographic resume:** You probably have seen a resume that utilizes mainly graphics and images to depict a job applicant's working experiences and skills; this kind of resume is called an infographic resume.

- **Targeted resume:** It is also possible for a job applicant to purposely design his resume for a specific job or industry; that is an example of a targeted resume.

| Figure 8.1 | Chronological resume template |

Include your phone number, email ID, and city and state of residence

CONTACT INFORMATION

_____

_____

Add a brief statement about your experience, skills, career goals, and accomplishments

SUMMARY

_____

_____

In a chronological resume, you must always begin with the latest experience

EXPERIENCE

1. Position and Company Name
   Duration (xxxx-xxxx)

   _____

   _____

2. Position and Company Name
   Duration (xxxx-xxxx)

   _____

   _____

Start with the latest and add only 2-3 relevant qualifications

QUALIFICATIONS

1. Name of the degree and institute
   Duration (xxxx-xxxx)

   _____

   _____

2. Name of the degree and institute
   Duration (xxxx-xxxx)

   _____

   _____

ADDITIONAL ACHIEVEMENTS
- _____
- _____

SKILLS
- _____
- _____

8.2.1 10 important steps for crafting a successful job application cover letter

Before any potential employers can examine your resume/CV to see your qualifications, skills, and experiences, the first thing their busy eyes will glance through is your cover letter. A cover letter is so important and you can view it as a gateway into a rare opportunity of getting your desired job. This is why you must pay undivided attention to it when drafting your own. A recruiter/ employer may show significant interest in a job application if the cover letter is well-prepared, insightful, and motivational. It is a fact that anyone can produce an effective cover letter that can move future employers to act swiftly toward considering them for the jobs/positions they have applied for.

Here are ten practical and equally helpful things you can do to craft a successful job application's cover letter:

1. **Have a consistent pattern:** Be consistent in the structure you are using in the cover letter. This entails that you should utilize the same font and font size. It is believed that fonts like Calibri, Arial, and Helvetica are quite easy to read. Make sure your font size is not below 10; the rule of thumb is to use a font size between 10 and 12.

2. **Include appropriate salutations:** A cover letter is usually formal, whether you are quite familiar with the recruiter or not. Hence, it should have the appropriate salutations or greetings such as "Dear Sir" or "Dear Madam". Use "Dear, Sir/Madam" if you don't know the gender of the recipient. It is very rude and improper to start a cover letter with "Hi, there!" or "Hey You!". Remember it is supposed to be courteous and formal.

3. **Address the cover letter to a particular person:** It is not every time you will know the names and titles of the company's officials that will receive and first review your cover letter. If the recipient is anonymous, a simple "Dear Sir/Madam" will do. However, in situations where the names of job applications' recipients are provided, the normal practice is to particularly address the cover letter to the person. You can begin your cover letter with "Dear Mr. Williams" or "Dear Ms./Mrs. Davies" if you know their names precisely. This approach creates a feeling of familiarity and respect, and it could move the recruiter/ employer to show an uncommon interest in your job application.

4. **Specify which position are you applying for:** A big organization often has many open positions/jobs running at the same time. If you don't specify clearly in your cover letter, you may be pooled with other undefined cover letters. This serious mistake can cost you the job because recruiters/employers can pinpoint exactly what job/position you are interested in.

5. **Exhibit your skills and professional accomplishments:** There's no space for you in a cover letter to highlight all your previous professional and personal achievements. However, you can still showcase your most important accomplishments that are related to the job/position you are applying for. For instance, if you are interested in the position of a project manager, you can make a quick reference to another project you have successfully managed in the past. This piece of information may pique the recruiter's interest in your application and head straight into your resume/CV to know more about you and your professional accomplishments.

6. **Assure recruiters/employers that you are ready:** Somehow, employers and recruiters can read between the lines if you are ready or not to take up the challenges posed by the jobs they are advertising. They can detect how serious you are in the choice of words and expressions written in your cover letter. While you are not expected to be quite aggressive or to use too strong expressions that could be misconstrued as rude and full of pride, you can select words and expressions or terminologies that can convince your future employers that you know what you are doing and can deliver when hired. This is the best approach to subtly assure your prospective recruiters/employers that they have nothing to worry about employing you.

7. **Use a winning template:** Chances are that you are drafting your very first cover letter and wondering what is the best way to do it. Use a winning template to draft your cover letter. The template will indicate all the most important parts that must go into your cover letter in order to make it score a high point when reviewed by potential recruiters/ employers. Understand this, though: It is not the design or beauty of the cover letter template that will make you get a job. It is the important and well-crafted detailed information you included in the cover letter as required by the cover letter. And you can find free cover letter templates online or you may decide to buy one from those selling nice cover letter templates online.

8. **Proofread and edit:** It is wrong to send a shoddily prepared cover letter to recruiters/employers. How about the typographical errors in them that could discourage a recruiter from going into discovering more in your resume/ CV? The purpose of a cover letter, essentially, is to nudge recruiters/employers into exploring more about you by

completely reading your resume/CV back to back. Though it is a top secret in talent acquisition, it is not rare that a busy recruiter can choose which job candidates to advance to the next round of employment procedure merely by judging the quality of their cover letters. For example, when Google or Apple, Inc. announces open jobs/positions, they could receive as many as one hundred thousand resumes/CVs. Do you think their recruiters will spend their productive hours reading that mountain of resumes/CVs? Never! They normally advance for further scrutiny job candidates with excellent experiences as described in their cover letters. It indicates that they will only be willing to examine the resumes/CVs of a handful of job applicants.

9. **Collect insider's knowledge:** On most occasions, job applicants will have minimal (little) or no insider knowledge about the companies they are applying to. Who is (are) the main official in charge of reading the cover letters and, of course, the resumes/CVs? What are their preferences when receiving cover letters? From which perspectives do they normally expect job applicants to demonstrate their levels of qualifications and professional achievements? To be honest, these are difficult pieces of information to discover. But if you have been lucky enough to have an inkling about how your targeted recruiter works, it is quite advisable that you should give it to them as they prefer to have it. Doing this simply increases your chances of being employed. Otherwise, you could attend job fairs and expositions organized by your targeted companies to know how they conduct their recruiting processes, and what exactly they want from job seekers.

10. **Get insights from current employees:** One of the sensible approaches for getting insider's knowledge or ideas that

you can use to embellish your cover letter is to contact current employees of the organization you wish to work at. Using their recruiting experiences, you could be advised about what to do and what not to do when crafting your cover letter that will be submitted to the organization for job application.

Figure 8.2 shows a sample cover letter. You can also download a ready-to-use cover letter template from the Online Resources available with this book.

Figure 8.2	**A sample cover letter**

NAME & CONTACT INFORMATION	→	**Your Name** Contact Information
SALUTATION	→	**Dear Hiring Manager/<insert name>,**
OPENING PARAGRAPH Begin by introducing yourself and enthusiastically explaining why you're applying for the job, your brief experience, and what you can bring to the table.	→	**I am reaching out to express my keen interest in the <insert position> role at <insert company name>. With my experience as <insert experience>, I am optimistic that my capabilities would greatly benefit your team.**
MIDDLE PARAGRAPHS Explain more about your experience, skills, and position of responsibility.	→	**Throughout my career, I have consistently demonstrated my proficiency in <insert information about skill/role>. My track record speaks to my ability to meet project deadlines, adhere to financial parameters, and satisfy expectations. Moreover, my adeptness in analytical thinking and problem-solving empowers me to identify and address potential risks.**
CLOSING PARAGRAPH Express enthusiasm and thank the employer.	→	**Thank you for considering my candidacy. I am enthusiastic about the opportunity to contribute my expertise to your esteemed organization and play a part in its enduring success.**
SIGNATURE	→	**Sincerely,** **Your Name**

8.3 Handling Your Pre-Interview Communication Like a Pro

Congratulations! You have scaled through the most difficult stage of your employment procedure by scoring an interview(s) with your great cover letter. Now it's time to handle all your pre-interview communication with a prospective recruiter/employer like a pro!

Highlighted below are some common sense steps you can take to appear like a true professional to your future employer/ recruiter:

- **Be prompt in replying to recruiter's/employer's messages:** Nowadays, most of the employment communication takes place by email. Therefore, if you've sent a job application to a company, it is sensible that you check your emails regularly. And any time you receive a message from the recruiter in the company, reply immediately. You can lose your opportunity of getting a job if it takes you so long to reply to a simple email from the recruiter/employer you have already contacted.

- **Be straightforward in your replies:** Don't go into writing lengthy replies when the recruiters need some clarifications from you. All you should do is reply with short, factual, and straightforward answers. Recruiters are normally busy people and don't have time to read your long, biographical tale.

- **Ask cogent questions:** Many jobseekers sometimes are afraid to ask their future employers some pertinent questions before attending the company's interview(s).

Understandably, most job applicants don't want to be unnecessarily pushy and bungle a rare opportunity to be hired. No one is advocating that you should be rude while asking questions; however, some questions are helpful, because they could help you prepare well for the interview(s).

- **Show courtesy:** Since potential recruiters/employers won't have a chance to meet you in person before the day of the interview, it is reasonable that you should be seen as courteous in all your dealings with them. Use appropriate language and tone in your emails. Be formal, and don't ever forget that your future employers/recruiters are still strangers who may be sensitive to a lot of things, including their perceived impression of your personality.

8.3.1 Expectations from employers during employment communication

The unique characteristic of employment communication is that two individuals are involved–the employer and the job applicant.[20]

Efforts have been made in this book to explain what is expected of a job applicant. This section dwells on certain actions employers must take to streamline communication with their prospective employees:

- **Clear instructions:** It is expected of employers (be it an individual or organization) to provide detailed information about the position or job they would like to fill. Some

20. Paryzch, P.A. (2000). *Employment communication. Massachusetts: South-Western Educational Publishing, p. 33.*

of the instructions include but are not limited to the full description of the job and its requirements, what kind of information is requested from the applicants, the methods of application (whether online or by mail), who to contact or send/address the application to, etc. Without providing clear instructions, most applicants would have no idea how to properly respond to a job advertisement.

- **Prompt response/guidance:** Employers should endeavor to respond promptly to messages they receive from job applicants to provide them with the appropriate guidance they would need to send in well-prepared resumes/CVs and cover letters.

- **Logistic support:** If available, employers should intimate job applicants about the possibility of paying for the applicants' transport fares to the interview venues when invited for an interview.

Quiz

1. To be gainfully employed, job applicants need to present their professional brands in a convincing way to their future employers. True or false?

   a. False

   b. True

2. When engaging in pre-interview communication with your prospective recruiters, you should _____

   a. Reply to their messages promptly

   b. Act rudely to them

   c. Not reply to their emails at all

3. This is one of the reasons job applicants don't necessarily ask questions when engaging in pre-interview communication with their future employers.

   a. They want to appear too pushy or desperate.

   b. They don't know how to ask questions from employers.

   c. They have over-confidence in themselves.

4. **What does this expression mean, "Be straightforward in your replies to prospective employers"?**

   a. It means that you should not send them long, windy replies.

   b. It means you should tell them what you ate for breakfast and lunch.

   c. It means you should accuse them of disturbing you with too many messages.

5. **It is important that job applicants should demonstrate their strongest skills and capabilities when reaching out to future employers/recruiters. True or false?**

   a. True

   b. False

6. **Which of these is NOT necessarily evidence of past work that employers may be looking for?**

   a. Job applicants' number of LinkedIn posts

   b. Job applicants' past projects completed in the same field

   c. Job applicants' accomplishments in similar fields

7. **In whichever way you are interacting with an employer pre-interview, let courtesy be reflected in all your actions. True or false?**

   a. False

   b. True

8. **Which category of job applicants can encourage busy recruiters to read their entire CVs/Resumes?**

    a. Those with beautifully designed cover letters

    b. Those with factual, well-written, and properly formatted cover letters

    c. Those with cover letters that are full of grammatical errors

9. **Cover letters are sometimes referred to as the "gateway" into a desired employment. You can get your dream job if your cover letter is done well. True or false?**

    a. True

    b. False

10. **Why is it always advisable to clearly state the exact job or position you are applying for in a company when sending a cover letter/resume to them?**

    a. To help recruiters know where to put you and your application among the pack of applications received

    b. To confuse the recruiters into giving you the job

    c. To tell a little lie about your accomplishments

Answers	1 – b	2 – a	3 – a	4 – a	5 – a
	6 – a	7 – b	8 – b	9 – a	10 – a

Chapter Summary

◆ It is surprising at times to realize people don't normally categorize "employment communication" as a part of business communication, but it is indeed an integral aspect of business communication.

◆ For job applicants, to win in a deeply competitive job market, you must learn how to perfectly present your professional brands to your future employers/ recruiters.

◆ Your prospect of getting your dream job begins with the quality and usefulness of your cover letter. There are some strategic things you should do to increase your chances of being invited for a job interview.

◆ Once you have been invited for an interview, do everything in your power to handle the pre-interview communication between you and your prospective recruiter/employer like a pro!

◆ Resumes/curriculum vitae (CVs) are a vital part of employment communication, and job applicants should be aware of which type of resume would fit the type of job they are applying for.

◆ Employers also have some significant actions to take to streamline their recruitment exercise, such as providing detailed instructions to the job applicants, promptly responding to messages from job applicants, and informing them of any pre-interview benefits that may be available to them.

This page is intentionally left blank

Chapter **9**

Business Communication and Customer Relationship Management (CRM)

Whenever the term "business communication" is mentioned, what naturally comes to mind is the kind of communication that occurs between a company and its customers. While this may be true to some extent, it has been shown convincingly in this book that there are several aspects to business communication. Notwithstanding, the interaction between organizations and their customers constitutes the largest percentage of business communication those organizations engage in. It is even suggested that businesses should frequently communicate with their customers; they should endeavor to answer those hundreds of emails, phone calls, and letters they get from their customers, whether they are complaints about products/ services they have subscribed to or receiving updates about new products/services releases.

The key learning objectives of this chapter should include the reader's understanding of the following:

- How to best interact with the customers

- Learning effective business communication for data collection

- Understanding the verbal and non-verbal cues for improving customer service

- Learning how to communicate with emotional and cultural intelligence

9.1 Customer Is King: Be All Ears To Your Customers

It is a common saying in the business community that the customer is king, even though this quote has never been attributed to one person. So, is it always true that the customer is king? Well, on one hand, a king has the power to decide what he wants to do with his time and how to spend his resources. Therefore, as king, customers have their money and time which could choose to spend on a company's products/services if they desire.

INTERESTING STATISTICS ABOUT CUSTOMER SERVICE

83% of customers agree that they feel more loyal to brands that respond and resolve their complaints.

65% of customers said they have changed to a different brand because of poor experience.

Source: khoros.com[21]

The two statistical figures above confirm in the strongest terms how customers view their relationships with the companies they patronize.

Surprisingly, 65% of customers have switched brands or stopped purchasing things from a brand they have had some poor experiences with. On the positive side, 85% of customers pledge their loyalty to brands that quickly respond and resolve their pain points. What does this connote? It indicates that organizations need to be all ears to their customers. They should often listen to them and promptly take drastic actions to resolve whatever problems they may be having while utilizing their products/services. Therefore, for an organization to have great customer service, it must put in place all procedures that would facilitate business communication between its employees and customers. It is not only enough to offer high-quality products/services that consumers will like, but also it is equally important to provide great customer service that will keep customers loyal and supportive.

Can a company lose all its customers over a certain period of time? Definitely. Any organization that fails to listen to its

---

21. "Must-Know Customer Service Statistics of 2023." Khoros. Accessed January 11, 2024. https://khoros.com.

customers' complaints stands to lose big in the ever-competitive marketplace.

To keep customers patronizing your products, pay attention to these common consumer complaints. Not only that, but you should also proffer useful solutions to their pain points and gladden their hearts.

Some common consumer problems are as follows:

- **How do I use this product?** Despite receiving a user's manual or guide when they purchase your product, some customers still struggle with how to use it. Listening to a very important complaint like this, a company can immediately respond with a piece of useful advice or solution that the confused customer can utilize to relieve himself/herself of whatever pain point he/she may be confronted with.

- **Why is your product not so useful for me?** At times, consumers feel dissatisfied with the products they have bought or services they have subscribed to simply because it is not doing what they expected it to do. It is the sole responsibility of the company producing that product to calmly explain to the frustrated customer how he/she can derive maximum satisfaction from using the product. Maybe the customer has even been using the product wrongly all the while, a little assistance from the company can change the customer's experience for the better.

- **How do I change or return your unused product?** This is one of the most annoying questions consumers ask. A lot of companies have not figured out how to help a disgruntled customer return or replace an unusable product. In certain cases, some companies' return policies are vague and unhelpful to their customers. In reality, some companies lose great customers at this point because those customers, who felt compelled to keep products they don't use or need, would perceive such companies as shady and fraudulent.

9.2 Effective Business Communication for Data Collection

Nowadays businesses rely on customers' data to carry out different analyses in order to detect if their business operations are growing and successful. And most of this data comes from regular communication between companies and their customers. Let's consider it this way: If there's no good relationship between an organization and its customers, it would practically be difficult to obtain the necessary information that the organization can process into useful data.

It is safe to say great customer service will engender genuine trust between the two parties. In this case, the customer will not be reluctant to release vital information about themselves to the requesting organization. It is quite understandable that there wouldn't be any wonderful relationship between a company and its customers if the communication between them has not been cordial, useful, and impactful.

Therefore, smoothly running an organization is all about designing and implementing effective business communication among all its stakeholders. Through effective business communication, it is possible for an organization to request any private information, to which its customers will willingly comply.

Highlighted below are some useful pieces of data that organizations can collect from their customers and act upon to better serve their interests:

- **A customer's personal information:** Due to privacy concerns, most of us will refuse to hand over our personal information to a company we do not particularly trust. Even when requested of us, we would do everything in our power to avoid giving it our name, address, phone number, etc. As the world struggles with the problem of scammers, everyone is protecting their personal information. It truly takes "trust" to be able to release your personal information to companies and that can only be built through prompt and cordial business communication.

- **A customer's credit approach:** Whether online or in-person, you may have been asked to answer a questionnaire or survey meant to determine your credit behavior or pattern. The truth is that if you don't trust the requesting organization, you will not be willing to answer those sensitive questions on the survey. For organizations, knowing their customers' credit behaviors is crucial to evaluating how much credit they can offer them, but before they can ask for such sensitive information their relationship with such customers should be wonderful.

- **A customer's preferences:** How would you feel if you were suddenly approached by an organization asking to know your preferences about certain products or services? It is true on most occasions that people will instinctively withdraw from that place where they are asked such an unexpected and private question. It happens all the time, and it is quite clear that it is only through the fostering of amazing relationships with customers that any organization can obtain its data without much hassle.

The following are the benefits of collecting and ethically using customers' data/information:[22]

- It contributes to an increase in data and improves its quality
- It helps build stronger customer relations
- It helps businesses provide personalized and relevant experiences
- It enhances operational efficiency
- It gives a competitive advantage over other businesses

9.2.1 How do organizations collect vital data from consumers?

Good customer service opens the door to satisfying relationships between organizations and their loyal customers. Technically, all relationships are built on great communication and goodwill.

Outlined below are some techniques companies adopt in obtaining their customers' information, and they all depend on effective business communication:

1. **Surveys:** It is not new for organizations to serve or send surveys out to their customers to gather some data they could make use of in making helpful business decisions. Surveys usually have some open—ended questions so that the respondents can provide information about their

---

22. Contributor, Stephan Miller - Guest. "What You Need to Know about Collecting and Using Customer Data." Capterra, September 28, 2023. https://www.capterra.com.

personal preferences. At present, surveys can be done anonymously.

2. **Newsletter and blog subscriptions:** Consumers may be asked to submit some information about themselves via newsletter and blog subscriptions. These include their names, addresses, telephone numbers, and locations. These pieces of data can be used to categorize or divide consumers into compact demographics.

3. **Social media:** Social media, as addictive as it is, can be utilized by companies to collect important data from consumers. It is not rare to see quizzes, questionnaires, and other data-collective, interrogative tools being embedded in a company's official social media posts for the purpose of gathering information from people.

4. **Customer orders:** A lot of vital data can be gleaned from customers' orders. While purchasing a product or subscribing to a service consumers are usually required to fill in some information about themselves.

5. **Promotions, competitions, and seasonal offers:** For centuries, organizations have long relied on promotions, competitions, and freebies to collect prospective or current customers' information.

6. **Transaction history:** Through a customer's transaction history, a company can obtain helpful data it could use in undertaking some analyses. The outcomes of such analyses may assist in the company's customer-centric decisions.

7. **Web-tracking capability:** Technology has also played a central role in supporting organizations' desire to track their customers' major activities online. To some extent, this action may not be totally legal since it may undermine

customers' privacy. However, many companies are still doing it—tracking the online activities of their customers in order to discover their preferences.

It is important to say that none of the above-mentioned data-collection processes would work if there wasn't any effective communication between organizations and their current and prospective customers.

9.3 Verbal and Non-verbal Cues for Better Customer Service

The truth is that every organization aspires to satisfactorily communicate with its customers so as to give them a wonderful customer experience. Unfortunately, the approaches taken by some of these organizations are not in any way effective.

Customer service experts believe that consumers respond favorably to both verbal and non-verbal cues aimed at giving them gratifying customer service.[23]

Let's take a look at some of these verbal and non-verbal cues.

9.3.1 Verbal cues

- **Sudden telephone calls:** Consumers often feel excited when they suddenly receive a call from a company that has sold things to them. Reaching out through unscheduled telephone calls can make consumers assume that the

---

23. Mero, J. (2015). *The Role of Non-Verbal Communication in Intercultural Business.* Munich: GRIN Verlag, 44.

company calling them does seriously care about them and is not just interested in their money.

- **Problem-solving meetings:** Whether it is impromptu or planned, online or in-person, consumers are elated that someone (a company in this case) values them and has called for a meeting to help them solve their problems, whatever it is. This elation could last for a lifetime as the customers feel the need to reciprocate in kind.

- **Home visits:** It usually excites consumers when some company's representatives come to their homes to talk directly with them on issues they may be having about certain products/services.

- **Events, expositions (expos), and lectures:** Through public events, expos, and lectures, companies can reach out to their customers to offer needed solutions or support in any areas they may be having issues with.

9.3.2 Non-verbal clues

- **Explanatory emails:** Whenever customers receive some explanatory emails from a company that attempts to tell them how best to use a product or enjoy the services they had subscribed to, it could fill them with a long-lasting admiration for the company. Hence, they will be happy to patronize such a company's products in the future.

- **Seasonal letters and cards:** Not long ago, organizations used to send seasonal, handwritten, or typed letters and cards to their customers. You could still see birthday letters, cards, and other greeting materials sent by a company to some customers in their homes. Even though email is fast replacing the letter-and-card tradition, it is still one of the non-verbal cues for engaging in productive customer service. Moreover, seasonal letters and cards offering greetings and discounts can also be sent via email.

- **Gifts/presents:** Organizations occasionally send gifts/presents to their customers to win their hearts. Everyone loves to be remembered and appreciated, and customers are human beings, too. When they are appreciated, they will demonstrate unusual loyalty to those organizations remembering them.

- **Freebies/Freemiums:** Giving consumers free things or services is still one of the most effective methods for getting into their heads. If the free service or product turns out to be of immense value to them, they could eventually become lifelong supporters of the company offering them.

9.4 Communicating With Emotional Intelligence

Verbal interactions between the organization and the customers, or between co-workers working together take place most effectively when the parties use emotional intelligence. What exactly is emotional intelligence? According to an article from the Harvard Business School, written by Lauren Landry, there are four aspects of emotional intelligence:[24]

1. Self-awareness

2. Self-management

3. Social awareness

4. Relationship management

---

24. Landry, L. (2022, September 19) Why emotional intelligence is important in leadership. Harvard Business Review. https://online.hbs.edu

Each of these aspects of emotional intelligence on their own carry with them an intentional way of being that includes openness and inviting and acknowledging others' opinions, beliefs, thoughts, desires, and suggestions. This means putting one's own emotions aside and being aware of the feelings and emotions of others. Managing relationships takes place when there is more positive interaction taking place than a persuasive one, when the exchange of information is taking place in an environment that is not threatening or provoking, and when the interaction is happening in a calm, safe, and secure manner even when the person may be angry or upset.

Roberta Moore, a Forbes Councils Member, in an article written about communicating with emotional intelligence, said there are five ways to be most effective and relatable.[25]

1. Listen and reflect before responding

2. Acknowledge and affirm

3. Use your empathy skills

4. Gather information through reality testing

5. Don't take things personally

Communicating with emotional intelligence and putting into action the most effective and relatable methods makes for great working relationships, both internally and externally. Talking about any topic in an environment that is welcoming makes it less stressful for all parties. This can only happen when all parties are sharing an interaction using emotional intelligence.

---

25. Moore, R. (2021, November 30) Say it with more emotional intelligence, Five communication tips for leaders. Forbes. https://www.forbes.com

9.5 Communicating With Cultural Intelligence

With the globalization of businesses and people relocating from places around the world, the most effective way to relate to such a diverse business and people society is to communicate with cultural intelligence. You may be wondering what cultural intelligence is, so here is the definition provided by Assistant Professor Echo Yuan Liao. Cultural intelligence is "the ability to function effectively in different cultural contexts."

Professor Liao says there are three interactive components to cultural intelligence: (1) Cultural knowledge, (2) Cross-cultural skills, and (3) Cultural metacognition (sometimes called Cultural Mindfulness).[26]

Cultural knowledge is more than learning about one's culture. It is understanding and appreciating how a culture expresses itself in various situations. In moments of disagreement or giving feedback, different cultures approach these situations differently. It is recommended that learning the approaches of different cultures take place by reading books and watching movies of diverse cultures, and if possible, visiting the countries and observing the locals.

Cross-cultural skills are a broad set of skills that are relational, tolerant of uncertainties and unfamiliarities, adapting one's behavior to match the cultural expectations, empathetic, and perceptual. These skills are operating simultaneously with deep respect while communicating and interacting with people from diverse cultures.

---

26. Liao, E.Y. (2015, March 24) Why you need cultural intelligence (And how to develop it) Forbes. https://www.forbes.com

Cultural metacognition/mindfulness takes place while taking control over one's thinking and paying attention to the other party's actions and reactions, reflecting on what went well in the interactions and what might have been said or done to have a better outcome, and placing oneself in the shoes of the other person.

In essence, communicating with cultural intelligence is operationalizing emotional intelligence among people of diverse cultures. Being aware of the cultural practices that drive the behavior, attitudes, opinions, beliefs, and expectations, and being willing to be open and accepting of them while communicating and interacting will no doubt create an open, welcoming, and inviting exchange of information, inspiration, and ideas that create a positive outcome for all parties.

It is important to always remember that the first step every business needs to take to do great in their customer service is to perfect or refine its business communication strategies.

Quiz

1. Organizations should be "all ears to their customers". True or false?

   a. False

   b. True

2. Which of these is a typical example of non-verbal cues for better customer service?

   a. Home visit

   b. Exposition

   c. Freemiums

3. How would consumers react to receiving a sudden, helpful phone call from a company they buy something from?

   a. Sad

   b. Excited

   c. Unimpressed

4. Which of these complaints is common among consumers who have already purchased a product from a company?

   a. How do I properly use it?

   b. When will you deliver it?

   c. What kind of product do you sell?

5. Consumers have to trust a company before they can release their personal information to it. This is because scammers may have unauthorized access to their sensitive data. True or false?

   a. True

   b. False

6. Which of these is NOT one of the primary personal data organizations could collect from consumers?

   a. Home address

   b. Telephone number

   c. Spending habit

7. Why are organizations interested in knowing consumers' credit behaviors?

   a. To know if they will be able to repay their credits

   b. To know if they own a house

   c. To know their personality

8. Freebies are free things companies give to their customers to win their hearts and/or encourage them to try out a new product. True or false?

   a. False

   b. True

9. Problem-solving meetings are an example of _____ for improving customer service.

   a. Non-verbal cue

   b. Verbal cue

   c. Neither verbal nor non-verbal cue

10. Doing customer service through sending gifts/presents to consumers is a total waste of money for organizations nowadays. True or false?

   a. True

   b. False

Answers	1 – b	2 – c	3 – b	4 – a	5 – a
	6 – c	7 – a	8 –b	9 – b	10 – b

Chapter Summary

◆ It is generally assumed, even in different business circles, that "business communication" is all about having engaging and meaningful communication between organizations and their customers. This is true to a large extent, and this chapter has comprehensively explained why it is so.

◆ Customers are king is a cliché that is still very much relevant in today's corporate world. Any organization that aspires to win the hearts of their customers and keep them loyal for a long time must recognize this fact.

◆ More so, for a company to collect much-needed data or information from its customers, there must be genuine trust and effective communication between the two parties.

◆ There are both verbal and non-verbal cues that organizations can adopt to improve their customer service.

◆ It is very important to communicate with emotional and cultural intelligence while dealing with customers to obtain the best results

Chapter 10

Social Media as a Vital Business Communication Tool

Companies have extended their tentacles from doing business on regular internet venues to social media platforms as well. The acceptance of social media as a business communication tool has opened new doors for expansive outreach to prospective customer base, which currently exists on social media platforms. No organization can overlook the promising prospect of finding a large number of customers among billions of people who use social media every day. Facebook alone boasts 2.934 billion active users in July 2022 and about 1.968 billion people reportedly used Facebook every day (Data Reportal). According to recent statistics, in 2021, the largest group on Facebook, which is estimated to be 19% of the total potential users, is men between the ages of 25 and 34.[27] While female users between the ages of 24 and 35 accounted for 13%, and male users between the ages of 18 and 24 are responsible for 15% of the total user population (The Social Shepherd).[28]

The key learning objectives of this chapter should include the reader's understanding of the following:

- Popular social media tools and platforms

- Key principles for social media management in business

- Use of social media and some ethical issues for business communication

10.1 Popular Social Media Tools and Platforms

Internationally, businesses take advantage of ten popular social media platforms to advance their business communication with their stakeholders, mostly their customers. These social media platforms have anywhere from millions to billions of active daily users.[29] This is something that offers great encouragement to companies that aspire to reach many potential customers as quickly as possible without necessarily breaking their bank accounts.

---

27. Datareportal (2023). *Facebook Users, Stats, Data Trends*. https://datareportal.com

28. The Social Shepherd (2023). *33 Essential Facebook Statistics You Need To Know In 2023*. https://thesocialshepherd.com

29. Negrusa, A.L., Rus, R.V., and Sofica, A. (2014). Innovative Tools Used by Business Networks and Clusters in Communication. *Procedia–Social and Behavioral Sciences*, 148 (6), p. 590. https://doi.org/10.1016/j.sbspro.2014.07.084

Highlighted below are the ten well-known social media platforms companies have discovered could be instrumental in broadcasting their brand uniqueness to their millions or billions of users:

Facebook

Founded on: February 4, 2004, by Mark Zuckerberg, Eduardo Saverin, Andrew McCollum, Dustin Moskovitz, and Chris Hughes

Number of active users: 2.93 billion (2022)

Usefulness in business: With a single Facebook post, an organization can reach thousands of current and potential customers/clients. Facebook also has tools for marketing/advertisement, business communication, networking, and other useful features. Facebook allows multiple forms to share your content including carousel posts, videos, short videos, and stories. Posting on Facebook can help generate traffic to your product page or website. Facebook marketing can also be used to advertise your products. Businesses are also using Facebook Messenger nowadays to reach out to their current and future customers.

Instagram

Founders: Kevin Systrom and Mike Krieger founded Instagram, which was launched officially in October 2010. It was bought by Facebook for $1 billion in 2012.

Number of active users: 500+ million (2022)

Usefulness in business: This social media platform affords the unique opportunity to post glowing pictures and videos of their products, services, and other business events they may be engaging in. In today's social media-driven world, Instagram marketing is one of the most important ways to gain customers and interact with the audience. These days, having a prestigious Instagram presence is a mark of a business's success. Instagram also allows for marketing through advertisements. Moreover businesses can keep in touch with their current and prospective customers via Instagram posts and direct messaging (DMs).

X

Founded in: X, formerly known as twitter was founded in March 2006 by Evan Williams, Biz Stone, Noah Glass, and Jack Dorsey. They launched the company in July 2006.

Number of active users: 206+ million (2022)

Usefulness in business: Businesses can post a few texts, several pictures, and videos about their products/services and other business activities/events. It also possesses marketing/advertisement, business communication, and networking features. A witty, engaging, and socially relevant. An X account is sure to attract potential customers.

Pinterest

Founders: It was founded by Ben Silbermann, Paul Sciarra, and Evan Sharp in March 2010.

Number of active users: 433 million (2022)

Usefulness in business: Businesses can expose their brands to millions of platform users by preparing their strategic brand messages as "pins" (photos/images). When Pinterest users click on the pins, they could be directed to the business's websites or e-commerce sites where sales and other transactions could take place. Pinterest also has tools for marketing/advertisement, business communication, networking, etc. Posting high-quality "pins" of your products/services would be a great strategy to market your business.

TikTok

Founders: TikTok was founded by Chinese tech giant ByteDance and was first released in September 2016 under the name "Douyin".

Number of active users: 800 million (2022)

Usefulness in business: Similar to Instagram, TikTok basically allows businesses to post videos of their products, marketing activities, and instructional videos about how to use those products. TikTok also has marketing/advertisement, business communication, and networking features.

LinkedIn

Founded in: It was founded in December 2002 by Reid Hoffman, Jean-Luc Vaillant, Lee Hower, Konstantin Guericke, Stephen Beitzel, David Eves, Ian McNish, Yan Pujante, and Chris Saccheri. It was bought by Microsoft in 2016.

Number of active users: 66.8 million (2022)

Usefulness in business: This is more like Facebook for business people and professionals to network with other like-minded entrepreneurs. They can post stories and content about themselves, their businesses, and their corporate activities. LinkedIn also has marketing/advertisement, business communication, and networking features. Having a LinkedIn presence is a mark of professionalism and will allow your business to be discovered by possible collaborators and prospective employees.

YouTube

Founded in: YouTube was founded by three former PayPal employees—Chad Hurley, Steve Chen, and Jawed Karim– in February 2005. However, Google bought the site in November 2006 for US$1.65 billion.

Number of active users: 122 million (2022)

Usefulness in business: This platform is basically used by businesses that want to post video content about their products and services. They could also post instructional videos that their customers can use. YouTube also makes it possible for companies to do video advertisements.

Reddit

Founded in: Reddit was founded by Steve Huffman and Alexis Ohanian, with Aaron Swartz, in 2005.

Number of active users: 50 million (2022)

Usefulness in business: Users of this social media platform can post content, news items, texts, and videos. It also permits businesses to do advertising and share some useful information that visitors to the site might like and click on.

WhatsApp

Founders The client application of WhatsApp was created by WhatsApp Inc., which was bought by Facebook in February 2014 for approximately $19.3 billion.

Number of active users: 2 billion (2022)

Usefulness in business: For businesses, WhatsApp is mostly utilized as a messaging and communication tool. Nowadays, users can post clickable links to videos and texts that they want to see. Festive greetings, reminders, and calls to participate in surveys can by WhatsApp.

Tumblr

Founded by: Tumblr was founded by David Karp in 2007 as a microblogging and social networking website.

Number of active users: 12.8 million active blog posts per day (2022)

Usefulness in business: Businesses can use this platform to microblog about their brands, products, and services.

Snapchat

Founded in: Snapchat was founded by Evan Spiegel, Bobby Murphy, and Reggie Brown in 2011 as an instant messaging app.

Number of active users: 557 million (2022)

Usefulness in business: Businesses can use this platform like WhatsApp, for instant messaging. There is also an opportunity to advertise their products on it.

10.2 Key Principles for Social Media Management in Business

Many companies that have rushed to embrace the possibilities of social media and opened accounts on some of the platforms have failed to reap the expected benefits of taking such an action. The major reason for this is that most of them do not necessarily actively manage their social media accounts. A large number of them do not have a social media management strategy in place.

Organizations that want to increase their social media followership and/or acquire new customers via the platforms should endeavor to undertake the following five social media management principles:

1. **Content strategy:** What is your content strategy? What kind of special messages are you trying to communicate to your current and prospective audiences (customers)? The content you post on social media should be relevant, concise, and contain appropriate keywords and call-to-actions. It is possible to recycle content as long as it is slightly refined and sensible to readers. Pictures or videos tend to perform well, since curious people will click on them and this may convert them to potential customers. Have a strong content strategy in place to avail the best benefits of social media.

2. **Consistency:** A company must be consistent in the messages and impressions it sends across to the outside world. Prospective customers will be discouraged from following and, of course, having financial transactions with businesses they deem inconsistent. It is also very important that companies post regularly on their social media business

accounts. Failure to do this may cause their social media followers to drop off one by one.

3. **Being trendy:** There's nothing wrong if a company follows the latest trends and shares trendy stories, messages, and content that will resonate with their social media followers. If the World Cup or Olympics is ongoing, posting content that is related to either of the sporting events will excite readers. This will give them the impression that the company posting such fresh messages is current and active.

4. **Responsiveness:** Sometimes people may ask questions, drop some hints, or even comment on a post a company has on its official social media page. It is wrong to leave those comments or questions unanswered. This is why organizations should have in-house or standby social media strategists or managers who have been trained to respond immediately to questions, comments, and even posts by strangers. In this way, a productive discussion can be started that may draw other people in, who also may excitedly contribute to the discussions.

5. **Striking a balance:** A company may be carried away thinking only about what it stands to gain from operating a social media account and then erratically bombard people with sales messages. This approach, on most occasions, is not effective at all; people don't exactly get attracted to salesy or pushy social media posts. However, if they are first given thrilling, well-thought-out posts, they may be interested in reading them. The company can cleverly put a few lines of sales messages in informative posts as well.

10.3 Use of Social Media and Some Ethical Issues For Business Communication

For organizations, using social media for business communication comes with some risks that could destroy the reputation of the affected organizations, if not properly managed. Therefore, companies should include risk mitigation in their social media strategies so that they don't find themselves in unforeseen trouble.

Here are some of the ethical issues companies can face while using social media to reach or interact with people:[30]

Breach of confidentiality: It is ethically inappropriate to reveal confidential information on social media. It doesn't matter whether an organization is trying to use such information to gain followership or not, it is expedient that all agreed-upon confidential matters must always be kept secret. Sometimes, results of surveys are released by companies on social media, but this can constitute a breach of trust on the part of the survey respondents/participants if their personal information is exposed on social media without following the due process.

- **Conflict of interests:** In a situation whereby the issue of conflict of interests may arise, it is practically reasonable not to put such information on social media. For instance, it will be truly unprofessional for a company to post damning reports of their competitors. If those maligned competitors are popular with people, it could lead to massive backlash

---

30. Clampitt, P.G. (2017). *Social Media Strategy: Tools for Professionals and Organizations.* California: Sage Publications, p. 23.

against the company attacking its rivals on social media with malicious posts.

- **False accusations:** Organizations should not falsely accuse either a person or another organization on social media. Peddling falsehoods to undermine others' integrity may cause social media users to avoid, like a plague, such a controversial organization that spreads lies about others.

- **Misleading claims:** Companies should never chase popularity or large followership on social media by providing misleading claims. They should not announce to their social media followers what is not true. For example, if a company claims that its product can help consumers solve their pain points, which is not actually true, that is a misleading claim, and the company could be sued by some disgruntled customers.

- **Intellectual property issue:** It is rational for an organization to only post content that is originally produced by the organization to avoid being accused of plagiarism or content theft. If anyone wants to use other people's content, the most appropriate thing to do is to acknowledge or reference the initial creators. This goes for blog posts, articles, pictures, and other materials.

Quiz

1. Social media platforms have nothing to offer businesses; it is simply another distraction for business managers. True or false?

   a. True

   b. False

2. Which of these social media platforms has more than 1 billion active users?

   a. Snapchat

   b. Facebook

   c. LinkedIn

3. Facebook allows businesses to advertise their products/ services to its billions of active users. True or false?

   a. False

   b. I don't know

   c. True

4. Plagiarism is a serious issue on social media. What does plagiarism mean in this context?

   a. Using another organization's content without referencing them as the original source of the content

   b. Posting on another organization's business page without permission

   c. Not hiring social media managers to help your business

5. **Which of these social media makes it possible for business users to post photos of their products and services as "pins"?**

   a. Reddit

   b. Pinterest

   c. YouTube

6. **When a company provides misleading information on its official social media page, one of the following could happen to it when its misleading information is discovered by consumers.**

   a. Its number of social media followers will increase dramatically

   b. Social media users will stop following or taking such a company seriously because of distrust

   c. More social media users will patronize the company's products/services.

7. **When a company intentionally releases private information/ data of its customers on social media without due process or permission, which of these illegal acts is committed?**

   a. Plagiarism

   b. Breach of confidentiality

   c. False accusations

8. Content strategy in social media management entails having a process for producing high-quality content, be it texts, images, or a combination of both. True or false?

   a. True

   b. False

9. Why do many organizations fail woefully to benefit from their venture into social media?

   a. They post messages every day.

   b. They lack a concrete and effective social media management strategy.

   c. They advertise too much on social media platforms.

10. What does it indicate that a company needs to be trendy in its social media posting?

   a. It means that by posting trendy content, social media users can believe that the company is current and active.

   b. It means that the company should cause some social problems so that it could be very popular on social media.

   c. I don't know

Answers	1 – b	2 – b	3 – c	4 – a	5 – b
	6 – b	7 – b	8 –a	9 – b	10 – a

Chapter Summary

◆ There was a mad rush for social media among businesses (companies), and this led to millions of business accounts being created on different social media such as Facebook, Instagram, Pinterest, LinkedIn, and so on.

◆ Organizations identified earlier on that these social media platforms could be a goldmine of opportunities for reaching billions of untapped markets and customer bases.

◆ Even though companies have been acquiring new customers via social media platforms, some of them still don't know how best to use social media due to their apparent lack of concrete social media management strategies.

◆ The use of social media also comes with an ethical baggage—in other words, if used inappropriately, an organization can lose its reputation as well as its customer base over time.

◆ So, we can conclude that social media platforms offer both opportunities and risks at the same time; so, companies must shrewdly approach the platforms to avoid getting into big trouble.

This page is intentionally left blank

Chapter **11**

Crisis Communication in Business

Crises can occur to any company/business at any time. These could be in the form of a massive drop in sales, a lack of qualified employees, a significant loss in market share, or even a natural disaster. It is the responsibility of the entrepreneur owning or running the business or the board of management of the company to quickly communicate these crises to every stakeholder associated with the company. Failure to do this could result in some unimaginable hindrances to production and hamper organizational growth because all stakeholders, at this moment, would be in a panic mode. Employees will not be motivated to do their routine work; suppliers won't be excited to deliver the much-needed raw materials to the affected organization; and more importantly, investors or financial institutions may withhold investing in such an organization that is badly affected by a crisis it may not survive. This is why a crisis communication plan is essential

> The key learning objectives of this chapter should include the reader's understanding of the following:
>
> - Crisis communication planning
>
> - The 5Cs of crisis communication (Care, commitment, competency, community, and continuity)
>
> - Turning a crisis into an opportunity

11.1 Crisis Communication Plan

As an entrepreneur, one of your attributes is taking calculated risks. It is not usually possible to speculate what the apparent outcomes of these risks would be. When they are successful, you should celebrate the achievement; but when they are not, they will possibly lead to a crisis. Though you are not expected to panic when a crisis does hit your business, all you need to do is bolster up your courage and find a way to resolve the crisis. If you don't do this on time your workers may be discouraged from doing their assigned duties; your investors will be livid that they had put their hard-earned money into your failing business; and your business associates may plan to cut ties with you.

The solution to this chaos is to promptly come up with a crisis communication plan if you haven't got any. This plan will be used to communicate to all stakeholders connected to your business to swiftly defuse the confusing situation, assuring all stakeholders that everything will be fine soon.

There is no specific pattern for designing and drafting a crisis communication plan because businesses encounter different challenges. However, it is advisable that your company's crisis communication plan should contain the following important elements:

- **It must be detail-oriented:** The crisis communication plan should include all the necessary details that are required to implement it. For instance, the purpose of the plan must be clearly stated. More so, the criteria that would be used in activating the plan must be distinctly defined or explained. For example, who has the power to activate the plan? When can such an action be taken? Is it before, during, or after the crisis has happened? It is also helpful to outline all the necessary procedures needed to activate the crisis communication plan.

- **Who are the crisis communication personnel?** A company may decide to carve out a new team among its existing employees tasked to plan, design, and implement the plan. The members of this important team should meet every now and then to discuss how to safeguard their company from being sorely affected by any crises. The team doesn't necessarily need to wait until a crisis occurs before acting. In fact, they should prepare a multi-year crisis communication plan, say for 3-5 years, and constantly update it as necessary.

- **What are the key messages?** Some of the key points or messages that could go into a crisis communication plan include but are not limited to the following:

  1. The information about the crisis itself—explaining the cause(s) of the crisis, has it ever happened before? If yes, what was done then to bring it under control?

  2. Explaining what impacts the newly occurred crisis has on the company's operations so far.

3. Describing what efforts the company has been making to address the issues (problems).

4. Highlighting how all the stakeholders' interests will be protected.

5. Offering a timeline for regular communication or updates about when the problems brought out by the crisis will be summarily solved.

- **What are the procedures for effective internal communication:** It is advisable to stipulate in the plan how employees and other stakeholders will be communicated when a crisis happens. Employees could receive messages directly to their email addresses or be given unrestricted access to the company's intranet. Sometimes a company may decide to reach out to all its stakeholders via the company's official social media account when a crisis happens.

- **Important contacts:** It is also very useful to have the applicable contacts listed in the plan. These could include media and emergency contacts. For example, the phone numbers of public health agencies, police, and the fire department. Equally, all stakeholders' and media's contacts are also necessary. The media may include TV, newspapers, radio stations, etc.

- **Appendices:** Some information may be put under the appendices, such as:

  I.   Employees' contact information

  II. Copies of the company's disaster recovery plans

  III. Internal and external communication checklists

  IV. Media contacts

    V.   Policies guiding social media posts and for granting interviews (to discourage granting unauthorized interviews)

    VI. Safety tips during a crisis

11.2 5 Cs of Crisis Communication

When crises occur, organizations should quickly adopt these 5 Cs of crisis communication described below:

1. **Care:** The first thing employees, customers, suppliers, investors, and other stakeholders of a company experiencing a sudden crisis want to hear is that they are going to be fine. This is because employees don't want to lose their jobs; investors don't want to see their hard-earned money vanish into thin air; and anxious suppliers won't like to be told that they can't get paid after scheduled deliveries! All these fears are real; because many organizations have folded up due to some unforeseen and unmanageable crises that occurred to them. Therefore, showing utmost care to your company's stakeholders when a crisis eventually happens is the first sensible step in keeping the situation under control. When sending out the first message about the crisis, it is reasonable to briefly mention the actions your company is taking to promptly address the dire situation (s).

2. **Commitment:** Organizations must demonstrate to their stakeholders that they are fully committed to decisively solving the problem (s) caused by the crisis, as quickly as possible. Not only that, but they must also regularly

communicate, to the stakeholders, the actions they are taking to swiftly ameliorate the situations and their expected outcomes. This singular action will bring hope and increase the trust level stakeholders have in the company.

3. **Competency:** When on an airplane and the pilots unexpectedly announce that the aircraft has developed a mechanical fault, despite the assurances they periodically receive from the pilots most passengers will still be afraid. However, knowing fully that the pilots have been properly trained and are competent to handle the dangerous situation may douse the fear in some passengers. The same thing is applicable when companies are managing crises that come as a rude shock to them. They need to show their employees, suppliers, customers, or investors who depend on them that things will soon be alright.

4. **Community:** There were instances when some organizations had poorly managed crises that had significantly affected them and their business activities. Considered a community, an organization must hold each of its stakeholders in high respect; this entails that everyone in the organizational community must be informed from time to time about how the community is trying to overcome the challenges it is facing. It doesn't help any stakeholder if a company that is struggling with a crisis chooses to keep employees, suppliers, investors, and other stakeholders in the dark. This will increase anxiety across the board and particularly weaken employees' motivation to do their assigned jobs. More so, as a community, everyone should collaborate on combating the problem.

5. **Continuity:** The primary reason all the four, above-mentioned steps are taken is to ensure that the company

affected by an unexpected crisis may remain in business. Even though a company's employees may be required to work from home or operate from a different facility, they must be constantly kept in the loop. Not only that, they must also be assured that the beleaguered company has no intention of shutting down. This will encourage all stakeholders to contribute their quotas in keeping the company operating, whether they are working from their respective homes or from another rented facility.

11.3 From Crisis to an Opportunity: Case Studies

Here, we shall take a cognizant look at how companies successfully steer themselves away from crises by improving their crisis communication procedures. They demonstrate a typical example of how any organization can turn its crises into opportunities.

1. **Samsung:** In 2016, Samsung was confronted with accusations that its Galaxy Note 7 was defective; the device was exploding into flames, as reported by some unhappy customers. Samsung immediately understood the negative effect such bad publicity would have on its long-formed image as a prominent maker of high-quality smartphones. To douse the tension caused by this news, Samsung utilized all avenues available to explain to disgruntled customers, apologize to the public, and offer to recall and replace faulty devices free of charge. More importantly, the company requested that its stakeholders should make products that comply with the industry standards and certifications. Samsung used traditional media as well as social media

to push out its appealing crisis communication until its customers got over that sad but serious experience and continued to buy Samsung products.

2. In 1996, Nike was accused of using underage labor (workers) to make its shoes in countries such as Indonesia and Vietnam. Workers as young as 14 years were reportedly hired by Nike's suppliers in those countries because they could pay them a very low wage, usually between $1 and $2. When the news broke, Nike quickly engaged in expansive crisis communication to reach out to everyone affected by this issue. First, they sent messages to their overseas suppliers to make sure that child labor was immediately ended—no workers should be under the legal working age in those countries. Second, Nike assured the U.S. government that it would apply the U.S. standards for Occupational Safety and Health Administration in its foreign suppliers' operations. Nike established a crisis management team that oversaw the implementation of all it promised the stakeholders in those foreign nations.[31]

Samsung and Nike were able to use their crises to turn their operations around. Had they chosen to be silent about those issues, they might have found themselves in a bigger problem as consumers shunned their products, which could have made them lose a lot of money (revenues).[32]

---

31. Corpwatch (2023). New York Times: Nike pledges to end child labor and apply U.S. rules abroad. Retrieved from https://www.corpwatch.org

32. Lopez, M. (2017, January 22). Samsung explains Note 7 battery explosions and turns crisis into opportunity. Forbes. Retrieved from https://www.forbes.com

Quiz

1. **When dealing with a crisis, an organization doesn't necessarily need a crisis communication plan. True or false?**

   a. True

   b. False

2. **When an organization is hit by a crisis or a set of crises, which of these is NOT technically true of the organization?**

   a. It may lose some revenues

   b. Its reputation will be affected

   c. Neither its revenues nor reputation will be affected

3. **Every crisis communication plan must include "key messages". True or false?**

   a. False

   b. True

4. **Why should an organization display some level of competence while handling its crisis?**

   a. Its stakeholders will increase their trust in the organization.

   b. To waste the time of its stakeholders

   c. To cast the blame for the crisis on its stakeholders

5. **It is a good practice for a company going through a crisis NOT to show any care to its employees, suppliers, and others. True or false?**

   a. True

   b. False

6. **Which of these documents CANNOT be put in the appendices of a communication plan?**

   a. The key messages

   b. Copies of social media policies

   c. Media contacts

7. **If well-managed, some crises could lead to better opportunities for most organizations. True or false?**

   a. False

   b. True

8. **What crisis did Samsung face in 2016?**

   a. Its Galaxy Note 7's batteries were exploding

   b. The sales of its Galaxy Note 7 increased

   c. The company didn't have any crisis in 2016

9. **Nike was accused of hiring child labor in its overseas shoe-making factories in what year?**

   a. 1996

   b. 2020

   c. 2017

10. How did Samsung handle its crisis then?

    a. It engaged all its stakeholders and the public in massive crisis communication

    b. It didn't do anything

    c. It stopped producing Galaxy Note 7

Answers	1 – b	2 – c	3 – b	4 – a	5 – b
	6 – a	7 – b	8 – a	9 – a	10 – a

Chapter Summary

◆ Crises happen, even when companies are not fully prepared for them, but the only way out is for such affected companies to come up quickly with a crisis communication plan to cover their unforeseen challenges.

◆ Even though the templates vary from one organization to another, every crisis communication plan must be detail-oriented, specific, and contain key messages to be communicated to all stakeholders.

◆ The 5Cs of crisis communications are care, commitment, competency, community, and continuity. An organization that hopes to overcome its crisis issue must embrace all these 5Cs of crisis communication.

◆ Sometimes crises can lead to greater opportunities, only if they are properly and decisively managed.